# • Cooking for Today •

## SIMPLE

## VEGETARIAN

## RECIPES

# • Cooking for Today •

# SIMPLE VEGETARIAN RECIPES

### ROSEMARY WADEY • SUE ASHWORTH
### CAROLE HANDSLIP • CAROL BOWEN
### PAMELA WESTLAND

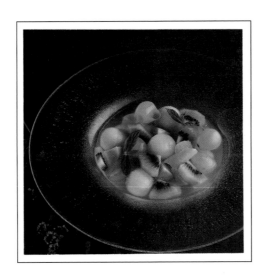

**WHITECAP BOOKS**

This edition published in 1997 by:
Whitecap Books Ltd.
351 Lynn Avenue
North Vancouver
BC V7J 2C4

ISBN 1-55110-701-5

Produced by Haldane Mason, London

Printed in Italy

Photographs on pages 12, 28, 42, 54, 68, 84, 98, 112, 126, 140, 156,
170, 184, 198 and 212 reproduced by permission of ZEFA Picture
Library (UK) Ltd.

*Note:*

Cup measurements in this book are for American cups. Tablespoons are
assumed to be 15ml. Unless otherwise stated, milk is assumed to be full-fat,
eggs are standard size 2 and pepper is freshly ground black pepper.

# Contents

**EVERYDAY DISHES** . . . . . . . . . . . . . . .**10**

**1**

Soups & Appetizers 13

Salads 29

Main Dishes 43

Light Dishes 55

Desserts 69

**VEGETARIAN DINNER PARTIES** . . . . . .**82**

**2**

Dips, Nibbles & Canapés 85

Appetizers & Soups 99

Main Courses 113

Vegetable Accompaniments 127

Salads 141

**VEGETARIAN BARBECUES** . . . . . . . . .**154**

**3**

Dips, Sauces & Marinades 157

Filled Things 171

Main Courses 185

Salads 199

Desserts 213

**VEGETARIAN CUISINE** . . . . . . . . . . . .**226**

**INDEX** . . . . . . . . . . . . . . . . . . .**236**

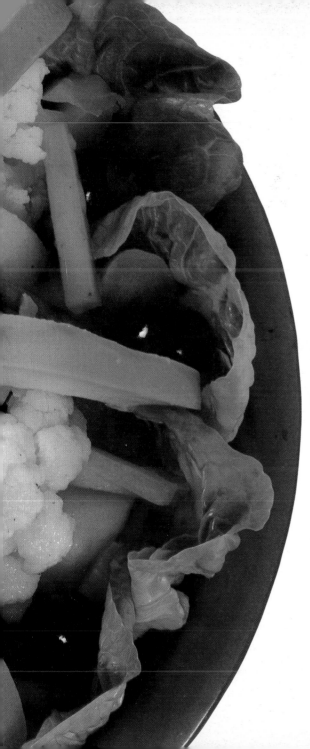

SIMPLE

# Vegetarian

RECIPES

In this inspiring book vegetarian cuisine is transformed into a delicious and exciting alternative to the more traditional menu. From exotic dishes like Nectarines in Almond Liqueur to appetizing twists on old ideas, such as Fruit Kebabs with Marshmallow Melts, the possibilities this book presents will change the mind of even the most confirmed meat-eater. The recipes for savory dishes are equally mouth-watering, ranging from quick and easy suppers to impressive formal dinners.

With a comprehensive techniques section containing details of the vitamin, mineral and fiber content of the various foods, *Complete Vegetarian Cooking* presents the reader with a complete guide to this most healthy and nutritious of cuisines.

**SOUPS & APPETIZERS**

•

**SALADS**

•

**MAIN DISHES**

•

**LIGHT DISHES**

•

**DESSERTS**

# 1

## EVERYDAY DISHES

# CHAPTER ONE

# Soups & Starters

Fresh vegetables are the basis of many wonderful vegetarian soups and appetizers. Bursting with flavor, they add variety and valuable vitamins and nutrition to meatless diets, and the flavor combinations are almost endless.

The recipes in this chapter are versatile. They make a delicious start to any meal, but several are substantial enough to be light meals on their own as well. Serve the Bean Soup on page 14 with chunks of crusty bread or wheat or corn tortillas, and the combination of beans with a grain will create what nutritionists consider a first-class protein to make a healthy light meal.  The creamy Yogurt & Spinach Soup on page 16 also makes a light meal on its own or is a perfect start to a spicy meal, where its mild flavor will provide an excellent contrast to the hotter flavors to follow.

One of the pleasures of a vegetarian diet is that it incorporates the flavors of foods from around the world.  These are recipes for a selection of international dishes, including the very quick and easy nachos from the American south-west, guacamole from Mexico and the chunky bean soup that is popular in Italy. The tortillas in this chapter form the basis of several Mexican-inspired dishes in the following chapters.

*Opposite: A loaf of fresh chunky whole wheat bread can turn a simple appetizer or soup into a filling first course, or even a light meal.*

# BEAN SOUP

*Beans feature widely in vegetarian cooking, and here pinto beans are cooked with a mixture of vegetables to give a spicy soup with an interesting texture. Serve with tortillas or crusty bread.*

STEP 2

STEP 4

STEP 6

STEP 6

SERVES 4

6 oz pinto beans
5¾ cups water
6–8 oz carrots, finely chopped
1 large onion, finely chopped
2–3 garlic cloves, crushed
½–1 chili, deseeded and finely
   chopped
4 cups chicken or vegetable stock
2 tomatoes, peeled and chopped finely
2 celery stalks, very thinly sliced
salt and pepper
1 tbsp chopped fresh cilantro
   (optional)

CROUTONS:
3 slices white bread
fat or oil for deep-frying
1–2 garlic cloves, crushed

**1** Soak the beans overnight in cold water; drain and place in a pan with the water. Bring to a boil and boil fast for 10 minutes. Cover and simmer for 2 hours, or until the beans are tender and most of the liquid has evaporated.

**2** Add the carrots, onion, garlic, chili and stock, and bring back to the boil. Cover and simmer for a further 30 minutes or so until very tender.

**3** Remove half the beans and vegetables with the cooking juices and press through a strainer or blend in a food processor until smooth.

**4** Return the strained or processed bean mixture to the saucepan and add the tomatoes and celery to the soup. Simmer for a further 10–15 minutes or until the celery is just tender, adding a little more stock or water if the soup is too thick.

**5** Add seasoning to taste and stir in the chopped cilantro, if using. Serve with the croûtons.

**6** To make the croûtons, remove the crusts from the bread and cut into cubes. Heat the oil with the garlic in a skillet and fry the croûtons until golden. Drain on paper towels. The croûtons may be made up to 48 hours in advance and stored in an airtight container.

## VARIATION

Pinto beans are widely available, but if you cannot find them or you wish to vary the recipe you can use cannellini beans or black-eye peas as an alternative.

STEP 1

STEP 2

STEP 3

STEP 5

# YOGURT & SPINACH SOUP

*Whole young spinach leaves add vibrant color to this unusual soup.*

SERVES 4

*2¹/₂ cups chicken stock*
*4 tbsp long-grain rice, rinsed and drained*
*4 tbsp water*
*1 tbsp cornstarch*
*2¹/₂ cups natural yogurt*
*juice of 1 lemon*
*3 egg yolks, lightly beaten*
*12 oz young spinach leaves, washed*
  *and drained*
*salt and pepper*

**1** Pour the stock into a large pan, season and bring to aboil. Add the rice and simmer for 10 minutes, until barely cooked. Remove from the heat.

**2** Pour the water into a small bowl and sift the cornstarch into it. Stir to make a thin, smooth paste.

**3** Pour the yogurt into a second pan and stir in the cornstarch mixture. Set the pan over a low heat and bring the yogurt slowly to the boil, stirring with a wooden spoon in one direction only. This will stabilize the yogurt and prevent it from separating or curdling on contact with the hot stock. When the yogurt has reached boiling point, stand the pan on a heat diffuser and leave to simmer slowly

for 10 minutes. Remove the pan from the heat and allow the mixture to cool slightly before stirring in the beaten egg yolks.

**4** Pour the yogurt mixture into the stock, stir in the lemon juice and stir to blend thoroughly. Keep the soup warm, but do not allow it to boil.

**5** Blanch the spinach leaves in a large pan of boiling salted water for 2–3 minutes until they begin to soften but have not collapsed. Tip the spinach into a colander, drain well and stir it into the soup. Taste the soup and adjust the seasoning if necesary. Serve in wide shallow soup plates, with hot, crusty bread.

## TO STABILIZE YOGURT

When stabilizing yogurt in the way described, it is important to stir it slowly and rhythmically in one direction only. Do not cover the pan, because any drops of condensation falling into the yogurt could cause it to separate. And do not be tempted to swish it about in first one direction and then the other.

**STEP 1**

**STEP 2**

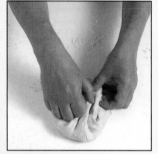

**STEP 3**

**STEP 4**

# TORTILLAS

*Tortillas are eaten with almost everything in Mexico in place of bread. Traditionally, they are made with masa harina (coarse-textured maize meal) but they can also be made with wheat flour: a mixture of maize meal and all-purpose flour also makes an excellent tortilla.*

MAKES 10

*WHEAT TORTILLAS:*
*10 oz all-purpose white flour*
*1 tsp salt*
*2 oz white vegetable shortening*
*5–6 fl oz warm water*

*CORN TORTILLAS:*
*5 oz all-purpose white flour*
*1 tsp salt*
*5 oz maize meal*
*1½ oz white vegetable shortening*
*about ¾ cup warm water*

**1** To make the wheat tortillas, sift the flour and salt into a bowl and rub the shortening into the flour with your fingertips until the mixture resembles fine bread crumbs.

**2** Add sufficient warm water to mix to a softish pliable dough; turn out on to a lightly floured work surface (counter) and knead until smooth (2–3 minutes). Place in a plastic bag and leave to rest for about 15 minutes. (Steps 1 and 2 may be done in a food processor.)

**3** Divide the dough into 10 equal pieces and keep covered with a damp cloth to prevent it from drying out.

Roll out each piece of dough on a lightly floured counter to a circle of 7–8 inches. Place the tortillas between sheets of paper towel as they are made to prevent them drying out.

**4** Heat a griddle or heavy-based skillet until just beginning to smoke. Brush off all excess flour from each tortilla, place in the pan and cook for 20–30 seconds only on each side until just speckled brown. They will quickly bubble from the heat and should be pressed down lightly with a spatula occasionally. Take care not to burn or brown them too much. Scrape any black deposits off the pan, they are burnt flour from the tortillas. Do not grease the pan.

**5** Wrap the tortillas in a dish cloth or place between sheets of paper towel to keep them pliable. When cold, wrap in plastic wrap if they are not to be used at once. They will keep in the refrigerator for several days.

**6** Corn tortillas are made in a similar way, except the flour and salt is sifted into a bowl, the maize meal is mixed in and then the shortening is rubbed in finely; continue as for wheat tortillas.

# NACHOS

*These are triangles of tortilla, deep-fried until they are crisp and topped with a variety of spicy mixtures and grated cheese to brown either under the broiler or in the oven.*

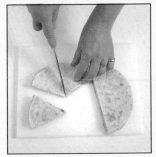

STEP 1

MAKES 30

5 wheator corn tortillas (see page 18)
oil for frying
1 red bell pepper, cored, halved and deseeded
10-oz jar tomato salsa dip
4 scallions, trimmed and chopped
4 tomatoes, peeled and chopped
1-lb can refried beans
6 oz sharp Cheddar cheese, grated
3 tbsp grated Parmesan cheese
chopped fresh cilantro, to garnish

**1** Stack the tortillas neatly and cut in half with a sharp knife, and then cut each half into 3 wedges to give 6 nachos from each tortilla.

**2** Heat about 1 inch oil in a large skillet until just smoking. Fry the pieces of tortilla – a few at a time – until crispy and lightly browned, turning once. Remove and drain on paper towels before transferring to cookie sheets.

**3** Put the bell pepper cut-side downwards into a broiler pan and place under a preheated moderate broiler until the skin is charred. Remove and leave to cool slightly. Peel off the skin and then chop the bell pepper.

**4** Put the chopped bell pepper in a bowl with the salsa dip, scallions and tomatoes, and mix together well.

**5** Mash the refried beans and spread an even layer over each nacho, then top with the tomato salsa mixture.

**6** Sprinkle with the cheeses and place under a preheated moderate broiler until the cheese bubbles. Alternatively, place in a preheated oven at 400°F for about 10 minutes until the cheese is bubbling. Serve hot or cold sprinkled with chopped cilantro.

STEP 2

STEP 5

### SERVING NACHOS

The choice of toppings for nachos is unlimited and they may be served hot or cold as a appetizer, a snack or an accompaniment for drinks.

STEP 6

# PALM HEART & PAPAYA VINAIGRETTE

*A really impressive first course, in which the colors complement each other as do the subtly intriguing flavors. Use either the Lime & Honey Dressing or the Chervil Dressing.*

STEP 1

SERVES 6

*1 small papaya, halved and deseeded*
*1 3-oz can palm hearts*
*1 bunch watercress*
*2 tbsp pine nuts, browned*

*LIME & HONEY DRESSING:*
*grated rind of 1 lime*
*3 tbsp lime juice*
*2 tbsp olive oil*
*2 tbsp clear honey*
*salt and pepper*

*CHERVIL DRESSING:*
*2 tbsp superfine sugar*
*1 tbsp boiling water*
*2 tbsp chopped fresh chervil*
*2 tbsp olive oil*
*3 tbsp lemon juice*

**1** Peel the papaya thinly and cut lengthwise into thin slices. Arrange on individual plates.

**2** Drain the palm hearts. Cut the palm hearts diagonally into rings and arrange over the papaya.

**3** Break the watercress into sprigs and arrange around the edge of the plates.

**4** To make the Lime & Honey Dressing, mix the grated lime rind and juice with the olive oil, honey and seasoning to taste.

**5** To make the Chervil Dressing, mix the sugar, boiling water and chervil together, then mix in the olive oil and lemon juice.

**6** Pour a little of the dressing over each salad and sprinkle the pine nuts over the top.

STEP 2

STEP 3

### PAPAYA

The skin of a papaya turns from green to an orange-yellow as it ripens, and should give slightly when pressed. When you slice one in half, you will find bright salmon-pink flesh with a mass of little grey seeds. The seeds are edible but are very hot and peppery. The flesh is delicious served simply with lime juice, but blends extremely well with other tropical fruits.

STEP 4

STEP 1

STEP 2

STEP 3

STEP 4

# GUACAMOLE

*This Mexican avocado dip is served as an accompaniment to many other dishes, as well as being enjoyed as a appetizer, with tacos for scooping it up. The chili content can be varied to suit your own particular taste by increasing the amount of Tabasco sauce used.*

SERVES 4

4–6 scallions, trimmed
2 large ripe avocados, quartered, stoned
  (deseeded) and peeled
1 tbsp lime juice
2–3 garlic cloves, crushed
few drops Tabasco sauce
2–4 tomatoes, peeled, deseeded and
  finely chopped
1–2 tbsp soured cream (optional)
salt and pepper
1 tbsp chopped fresh cilantro or chives

**1** Put the scallions into a food processor and finely chop. Cut the avocado into slices, add to the food processor and work until smooth. Alternatively, chop the onions finely with a knife and mash the avocados and onions together thoroughly with a fork.

**2** Add the lime juice, garlic and Tabasco sauce to the avocado mixture and work or mash until smoothly blended. Turn out into a bowl.

**3** Stir in the chopped tomatoes and the  soured cream, if using, and season the mixture to taste. Then mix in half the chopped fresh cilantro or chives.

**4** Turn the guacamole into a serving bowl. If it is not to be used immediately, bury one of the avocado seeds in it as this will help it to keep its color. Cover the guacamole tightly with plastic wrap until you are ready to use it. Remove the avocado seed at the last minute, and sprinkle with the remaining cilantro or chives.

**5** Serve as a starter with tacos or tortillas, or use with other ingredients as a topping for tortillas or as part of other recipes.

## MASHING AVOCADOS

If you are making guacamole without the aid of a food processor, use very ripe avocados or they will not mash easily to give a creamy texture to the guacamole.

STEP 1

STEP 2

STEP 4

STEP 5

# STUFFED EGGPLANT ROLLS

*Long slices of eggplant are blanched and stuffed with a savory rice and nut mixture, and baked in a piquant tomato and wine sauce to serve cold as a starter.*

**SERVES 8**

3 eggplants, total weight about 1½ lb
⅓ cup mixed long-grain and wild rice
4 scallions, trimmed and thinly sliced
3 tbsp chopped cashew nuts or toasted
   chopped hazelnuts
2 tbsp capers
1 garlic clove, crushed
2 tbsp grated Parmesan cheese
1 egg, beaten
1 tbsp olive oil
1 tbsp balsamic vinegar
2 tbsp tomato paste
⅔ cup water
⅔ cup white wine
salt and pepper
coriander cilantro sprigs, to garnish

**1** Cut off the stem end of each eggplant, then cut off and discard a strip of skin from alternate sides of each eggplant. Cut each eggplant into thin slices to give a total of 16 slices.

**2** Blanch the eggplant slices in boiling water for 5 minutes, then drain on paper towels.

**3** Cook the wild rice in boiling salted water for about 50 minutes, adding the long-grain rice for the last 12 minutes of cooking time. Drain and place in a bowl. Add the scallions, nuts, capers, garlic, cheese, egg, salt and pepper, and mix well.

**4** Spread a thin layer of rice mixture over each slice of eggplant and roll up carefully, securing with a wooden toothpick. Place the rolls in a greased ovenproof dish and brush each one with the olive oil.

**5** Combine the vinegar, tomato paste and water, and pour over the eggplant rolls. Cook in a preheated oven at 350°F for about 40 minutes until tender and most of the liquid has been absorbed. Transfer the rolls to a serving dish.

**6** Add the wine to the pan juices and heat gently until the sediment loosens and then simmer gently for 2–3 minutes. Adjust the seasoning and strain over the eggplant rolls. Leave until cold and then chill thoroughly. Garnish with sprigs of cilantro before serving.

# CHAPTER TWO

# *Salads*

A freshly made salad is always a welcome addition to any
vegetarian meal and often makes an ideal appetizer. The first
course of any meal should be tantalizing to the taste-buds
and not too heavy, so these salads fit the bill perfectly. They
provide an infinite variety of tastes, textures and colors,
and a superb opportunity for the cook to display an
imaginative flair and get the meal off to a good start by pleasing
the eye as well as the appetite. They also make wonderful light
meals, and you will find some ideas here versatile enough to serve
as dips and for picnics.

Use pretty dishes to complement your chosen salad: scallop shells,
for example, or other interesting shapes; or perhaps glass plates,
which can be plain, colored, decorated or frosted. Take care
over the decoration and garnish, and use sprigs of fresh herbs
where possible. Serve a first course salad with Melba toast
or with one of the many exciting Mediterranean breads
available which are flavored with oils and aromatic herbs.
These are particularly suitable, as they can be served warm, in
satisfying chunks, attractively presented in a basket.

*Opposite: Use the freshest
vegetables in contrasting
colors for a striking effect.
Vivid reds and greens are
particularly effective.*

# TOMATO SALSA

*Serve this attractive-looking salad with all its delicious flavors as anything from a dip to a relish and as an accompaniment to almost any dish.*

**STEP 1**

**STEP 2**

**STEP 3**

**STEP 4**

SERVES 4

4 ripe tomatoes
1 medium red-skinned onion or 6 scallions
1–2 garlic cloves, crushed (optional)
2 tbsp chopped fresh cilantro
$^1/_2$ red or green chili (optional)
finely grated rind of $^1/_2$–1 lemon or lime
1–2 tbsp lemon or lime juice
pepper

**1** Chop the tomatoes fairly finely and evenly, and put into a bowl. They must be firm and a good strong red color for the best results, but if preferred, they may be peeled by placing them in boiling water for about 20 seconds and then plunging into cold water. The skins should then slip off easily when they are nicked with a knife.

**2** Peel and slice the red onions thinly, or trim the scallions and cut into thin slanting slices; add to the tomatoes with the garlic and cilantro and mix lightly.

**3** Remove the seeds from the red or green chili, if using, chop the flesh very finely and add to the salad. Treat the chilies with care; do not touch your eyes or face after handling them until you

have washed your hands thoroughly. Chili juices can burn.

**4** Add the lemon or lime rind and juice to the salsa, and mix well. Transfer to a serving bowl and sprinkle with pepper.

### VARIATION

If you don't like the distinctive flavor of fresh cilantro, you can replace it with flat-leaf parsley instead.

### STORING

This salad may be covered with plastic wrap and stored in the refrigerator for up to 36 hours before use.

# WALDORF SLAW

*This salad combines the best of a Waldorf salad and a coleslaw in a tart yogurt dressing with an attractive garnish of carrot sticks.*

STEP 1

SERVES 4–6

4 celery stalks, preferably green
¼ white cabbage (about 8 oz)
⅓ cup raisins
½ cup walnut pieces
4–6 scallions, trimmed and cut into thin
    slanting slices
2 green-skinned eating apples
2 tbsp lemon or lime juice
4 tbsp thick mayonnaise
2 tbsp natural yogurt or natural
    fromage frais
2 tbsp vinaigrette
salt and pepper
2 carrots, trimmed, to garnish

**1** Cut the celery into narrow slanting slices. Remove the core from the cabbage and finely shred either by hand or using the slicing blade of a food processor.

**2** Put the celery, cabbage, raisins, walnut pieces and scallions into a bowl and mix together.

**3** Quarter and core the apples and slice thinly, or cut into dice. Put into a bowl with the lemon or lime juice and toss until completely coated. Drain and add to the other salad ingredients.

**4** Whisk together the mayonnaise, yogurt or fromage frais and vinaigrette, and season well. Add to the salad and toss evenly through it. Turn into a serving bowl.

STEP 3

**5** To make the garnish, cut the carrots into very narrow julienne strips about 2 inches in length and arrange around the edge of the salad.

**6** Cover with plastic wrap and chill until ready to serve.

STEP 4

### VARIATION

This salad can be made using red cabbage for a change, and firm pears can be used in place of the apples.

STEP 5

STEP 3

STEP 4

STEP 5

STEP 6

# MEXICAN SALAD

*Cooked new potatoes and blanched cauliflower are combined with carrots, olives, capers and gherkins in a tangy mustard dressing for a salad suitable as an accompaniment or as a main dish.*

SERVES 4

*1 lb small new potatoes, scraped
salt
8 oz small cauliflower florets
1–2 carrots, peeled
3 large gherkins
2–3 scallions, trimmed
1–2 tbsp capers
12 pitted black olives
1 iceberg lettuce or other lettuce leaves*

*DRESSING:
1¹/₂–2 tsp Dijon mustard
1 tsp sugar
2 tbsp olive oil
4 tbsp thick mayonnaise
1 tbsp wine vinegar
salt and pepper*

*TO GARNISH:
1 ripe avocado
1 tbsp lime or lemon juice*

**1** Cook the potatoes in salted water until they are just tender; drain, cool and either dice or slice. Cook the cauliflower in boiling salted water for 2 minutes. Drain, rinse in cold water and drain again.

**2** Cut the carrots into narrow julienne strips and mix with the potatoes and cauliflower.

**3** Cut the gherkins and scallions into slanting slices, then add them to the salad together with the capers and black olives.

**4** Arrange the lettuce leaves on a plate or in a bowl and spoon the salad over the lettuce.

**5** To make the dressing, whisk all the ingredients together until completely emulsified. Drizzle the dressing over the salad.

**6** Cut the avocado into quarters, then remove the seed and peel. Cut into slices and dip immediately in the lime or lemon juice. Use to garnish the salad just before serving.

## USING DIFFERENT VEGETABLES

This salad is a very versatile one – you can incorporate or substitute a variety of other vegetables according to your own personal preference.

# PROVENCAL TOMATO & BASIL SALAD

*These extra-large tomatoes make an excellent salad, especially when sliced and layered with fresh basil, garlic, kiwi fruit and onion rings together with dressed baby new potatoes.*

STEP 2

STEP 3

STEP 4

STEP 5

SERVES 6–8

1 lb tiny new or salad potatoes, scrubbed
4–5 extra-large tomatoes
2 kiwi fruit
1 onion, very thinly sliced
2 tbsp roughly chopped fresh basil leaves
fresh basil leaves, to garnish

DRESSING:
4 tbsp virgin olive oil
2 tbsp balsamic vinegar
1 garlic clove, crushed
2 tbsp mayonnaise or soured cream
salt and pepper

**1** Cook the potatoes in their skins in salted water for 10–15 minutes until they are just tender, then drain thoroughly.

**2** To make the dressing, whisk together the oil, vinegar, garlic and seasoning until completely emulsified. Transfer half of the dressing to another bowl and whisk in the mayonnaise or soured cream.

**3** Add the creamy dressing to the warm potatoes and toss thoroughly, then leave until cold.

**4** Wipe the tomatoes and slice thinly. Peel the kiwi fruit and cut into thin slices. Layer the tomatoes with the kiwi fruit, slices of onion and chopped basil in a fairly shallow dish, leaving a space in the centre for the potatoes.

**5** Spoon the potatoes in their dressing into the centre of the tomato salad.

**6** Drizzle a little of the plain dressing over the tomatoes, or serve separately in a bowl or jug. Garnish the salad with fresh basil leaves. Cover the dish with plastic wrap and chill until ready to serve.

### TOMATOES

Ordinary tomatoes can be used for this salad, but make sure they are firm and bright red. You will need 8–10 tomatoes.

# CAESAR SALAD

*This salad is traditionally made with romaine lettuce, although any crisp variety can be used.*

STEP 3

STEP 4

STEP 5

STEP 7

SERVES 4

4 tbsp olive oil
2 tbsp lemon juice
2 garlic cloves, crushed
1 tsp Worcestershire sauce
1 egg
6 quail's eggs
1 large romaine lettuce
1 oz Parmesan cheese
2 slices bread, crusts removed
4 tbsp corn oil
salt and pepper

**1** Mix together the olive oil, lemon juice, garlic and Worcestershire sauce with salt and pepper to taste. Put the single egg in a blender or food processor and blend for 30 seconds. Add the oil mixture gradually through the feeder tube until the dressing thickens slightly.

**2** If you do not have a food processor, you can make the dressing using a hand-held electric whisk, or a hand whisk. Put the egg in a small bowl and whisk in the garlic, Worcestershire sauce and seasoning. Gradually whisk in the oil and finally add the lemon juice.

**3** Boil the quail's eggs for 5 minutes, then plunge them into cold water to cool. Crack the shells and remove the eggs very carefully, then cut the eggs into quarters.

**4** Tear the lettuce into manageable-sized pieces and put into a salad bowl with the quail's eggs.

**5** Using a potato peeler, shave peelings off the Parmesan cheese.

**6** Cut the bread into ¼-inch cubes and fry in the corn oil until golden. Drain well on paper towels.

**7** Pour the dressing over the salad and toss thoroughly, then sprinkle the croûtons and Parmesan shavings over the top.

# GARDEN SALAD

*This chunky salad includes tiny new potatoes tossed in a minty dressing, and has a mustard dip for dunking.*

STEP 1

SERVES 6–8

1 lb tiny new or salad potatoes
4 tbsp vinaigrette made with olive oil
2 tbsp chopped fresh mint
6 tbsp soured cream
3 tbsp thick mayonnaise
2 tsp balsamic vinegar
1½ tsp coarse-grain mustard
½ tsp creamed horseradish
good pinch brown sugar
8 oz broccoli florets
4 oz sugar snap peas or snow
  peas, trimmed
2 large carrots
4 celery stalks
1 yellow or orange bell pepper,
  halved, cored and deseeded
1 bunch scallions, trimmed
  optional)
1 head endive
salt and pepper

**1** Cook the potatoes in boiling salted water for about 10 minutes until just tender. While they cook, combine the vinaigrette and mint. Drain the potatoes thoroughly, add to the dressing while they are still hot, toss well and leave until cold, giving an occasional stir.

**2** To make the dip, combine the soured cream, mayonnaise, vinegar, mustard, horseradish, sugar and seasoning.

**3** Cut the broccoli into bite-sized florets and blanch for 2 minutes in boiling water. Drain and toss immediately in cold water; when cold, drain thoroughly.

**4** Blanch the sugar snap peas or snow peas in the same way but only for 1 minute. Drain, rinse in cold water and drain again.

**5** Cut the carrots and celery into sticks measuring about $2\frac{1}{2} \times \frac{1}{2}$ inch; and slice the bell pepper or cut into cubes. Cut off some of the green part of the scallions, if using, and separate the endive leaves.

**6** Arrange the vegetables attractively in a fairly shallow bowl with the potatoes piled up in the centre. Cover with plastic wrap until ready to serve. Serve the dip separately.

STEP 2

STEP 5

STEP 6

# CHAPTER THREE

# *Main Dishes*

Here's a selection of recipes suitable for all occasions, whether you are entertaining or cooking for your family. Even your meat-eating friends will be happy with these dishes. Traditional vegetarian favourites such as nutburgers are here, as well as more exotic dishes, such as spiced Indian vegetables with coconut and a spicy Mexican mixed vegetable dish that is just as delicious served as an accompaniment as well.

When you are planning a vegetarian meal, select your main dish first and then decide on the accompaniment. Plan dishes that provide a balance of textures and flavors and use a variety of ingredients. Busy cooks will also want to think about including dishes that can be cooked ahead in their menu.

Always use vegetables that are at their peak so these dishes will have the maximum amount of flavors. Any vegetables that are beginning to become limp or look tired belong in the stockpot rather than in main course dishes.

Opposite: *Always use fresh ingredients that are at the peak for maximum flavor. Select dishes that feature a variety of fruits and vegetables so you have a mixture of textures and tastes.*

# AVIYAL

*This is a mixture of vegetables lightly flavored with coconut, ginger and spices to give an Indian flavor. As well as being a delicious main course, this also makes a good accompaniment to curries.*

STEP 1

**SERVES 4**

2²/₃ cups shredded coconut or
   4 oz creamed coconut
1¹/₄ cups boiling water
2 tbsp sunflower oil
1 oz ginger root, grated
2 onions, chopped finely
1 garlic clove, crushed
2 tsp ground coriander
1 tbsp garam masala
1 tsp turmeric
2 green bell peppers, cored, deseeded and
   sliced in thin rings
1 red or yellow bell pepper, cored, deseeded
   and sliced in thin rings
2 carrots, cut into julienne strips
1 green chili, cored, deseeded and sliced
   (optional)
4–6 oz French or fine beans, cut into
   3-inch lengths
6 oz green broccoli, divided into florets
3 tomatoes, peeled, quartered and
   deseeded
salt and pepper

**1** Soak the coconut in the boiling water for 20 minutes, then process in a food processor until smooth, or blend the creamed coconut with the boiling water until smooth.

**2** Heat the oil in the wok, swirling it around until really hot. Add the ginger, onions and garlic and stir-fry for 2–3 minutes until they are beginning to colour slightly.

**3** Add the coriander, garam masala and turmeric and continue to stir-fry for a few minutes then add the peppers, carrots, chili, beans, broccoli and tomatoes, and stir-fry for 4–5 minutes, turning the heat down a little.

**4** Add the coconut and plenty of seasoning and bring to the boil. Continue to simmer and stir-fry for about 5–8 minutes, until tender but still with a bite to the vegetables.

**5** Serve as a main dish with boiled rice or noodles, or as an accompaniment to a curry.

STEP 2

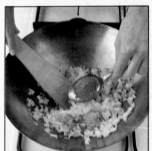
STEP 3

STEP 4

STEP 2

STEP 3

STEP 4

STEP 5

# WARM PASTA WITH BASIL VINAIGRETTE

*All the ingredients of pesto sauce are included here – basil, pine nuts, Parmesan cheese and olive oil. Sun-dried tomatoes and olives complete this delicious salad, which is just as tasty served cold.*

SERVES 4

*8 oz pasta spirals*
*4 tomatoes*
*¹/₂ cup black olives*
*¹/₄ cup sun-dried tomatoes*
*2 tbsp pine nuts, browned*
*2 tbsp Parmesan cheese shavings*
*fresh basil sprig, to garnish*

*BASIL VINAIGRETTE:*
*4 tbsp chopped fresh basil*
*1 garlic clove, crushed*
*2 tbsp grated Parmesan cheese*
*4 tbsp olive oil*
*2 tbsp lemon juice*
*pepper*

**1** Cook the pasta in boiling salted water for 10–12 minutes until just tender. Drain and rinse well in hot water, then drain again thoroughly.

**2** To make the vinaigrette, mix the basil, garlic, Parmesan cheese, olive oil, lemon juice and pepper together with a whisk until blended.

**3** Put the pasta into a bowl, pour over the basil vinaigrette and toss thoroughly.

**4** Skin the tomatoes and cut into wedges. Halve and pit the olives and slice the sun-dried tomatoes.

**5** Add them all to the pasta and mix together thoroughly. Transfer to a salad bowl and scatter the pine nuts and Parmesan shavings over the top. Serve warm, garnished with a sprig of basil.

## SUN-DRIED TOMATOES

Sun-dried tomatoes are, as their name indicates, tomatoes that have been halved and dried in the sun, leaving a wrinkled specimen with an extremely rich, concentrated flavor. They are usually covered with oil, and herbs and garlic are added to give extra flavor. When added to a sauce or salad they impart an added depth of flavor, and are also delicious eaten straight from the jar with a chunk of fresh bread.

# MEXICAN RICE

*This is a traditional way of cooking rice in Mexico. Onions, garlic, tomatoes, chilies and vegetables are added to the rice and cooked in a chicken or vegetable stock to make a filling dish.*

STEP 2

SERVES 6

1½ cups long-grain rice
3 tbsp oil
1 large onion, chopped
½ chili, deseeded and finely chopped
2 large garlic cloves, crushed
4 tomatoes (about 8 oz), peeled and chopped
3½ cups chicken or vegetable stock
4 oz frozen peas (optional)
salt and pepper
chopped fresh cilantro or parsley, to garnish

**1** Put the rice in a heatproof bowl, cover with boiling water and leave to rest for 10 minutes, then drain very thoroughly.

**2** Heat the oil in a pan, add the rice and fry gently, stirring almost constantly for about 5 minutes or until just beginning to color.

**3** Add the onion, chili, garlic, tomatoes and carrots, and continue to cook for a minute or so before adding the stock and bringing to a boil.

**4** Stir the rice well, cover the pan and simmer gently for 20 minutes without removing the lid.

**5** Stir in the peas, if using, and the seasoning. Continue to cook, covered, for about 5 minutes, or until all the liquid has been absorbed and the rice is tender.

**6** If time allows, leave the covered pan to rest for 5–10 minutes, then fork up the rice and serve sprinkled generously with chopped fresh cilantro or parsley.

STEP 3

STEP 5

### NOTE

The chili content of this dish can be increased to give a hotter taste, but be warned – once it has been added, it cannot be removed!

STEP 6

STEP 1

STEP 2

STEP 3

STEP 4

# NUTBURGERS WITH CHEESE

*A delicious mixture of chopped nuts, onion, garlic, herbs, carrot and Parmesan cheese shaped into small balls, dipped in egg and crumbs to fry and serve cold.*

MAKES 12

1 onion, finely chopped
1 garlic clove, crushed
1 tbsp olive oil
¼ cup all-purpose flour
½ cup vegetable stock or milk
2 cups chopped mixed nuts (including
    cashews, almonds, hazelnuts
    and walnuts)
1 cup fresh breadcrumbs
2 carrots, grated coarsely
1 tbsp chopped fresh parsley
1 tbsp dried thyme
2 tbsp grated Parmesan cheese
1 tbsp lemon juice
1 tsp vegetable extract
1 egg, beaten
dried breadcrumbs
salt and pepper
oil for deep-frying (optional)
mixed salad greens,
    to serve

**1** Fry the onion and garlic gently in the oil until soft. Stir in the flour and cook for 1–2 minutes. Add the stock or milk gradually and bring to aboil.

**2** Remove from the heat and stir in the nuts, breadcrumbs, carrots, herbs, Parmesan cheese, lemon juice,

vegetable extract and seasoning. Leave until cold.

**3** Divide the mixture into 12 and roll into even-sized balls.

**4** Dip each piece first in beaten egg and then coat in breadcrumbs.

**5** Place on a well greased cookie sheet and bake in a preheated oven at 350°F for about 20 minutes, or until lightly browned and crisp. Alternatively, deep-fry in oil heated to 350°F for 3–4 minutes until golden brown. The oil is at the correct temperature for deep-frying when a cube of bread browns in it in 30 seconds.

**6** Drain on crumpled paper towels, then, when cold, arrange on a bed of salad greens. Cover with plastic wrap or foil until ready to serve.

### VARIATION

These nutburgers can be made into miniature bite-sized balls if preferred, and they make excellent cocktail snacks.

# SWEET & SOUR VEGETABLES

*Make your own choice of vegetables from the suggested list, including scallions and garlic. For a hotter, spicier sauce, add chili sauce.*

STEP 1

**SERVES 4**

5–6 vegetables from the following:
1 bell pepper, red, green or yellow, cored, deseeded and sliced
125 g/4 oz French beans, cut into 2–3 pieces
125 g/4 oz snow peas, cut into 2–3 pieces
8 oz green broccoli or cauliflower, divided into tiny florets
8 oz zucchini cut into thin 2-inch lengths
6 oz carrots, cut into julienne strips
4 oz baby corn, thinly sliced
2 leeks, thinly sliced and cut into matchsticks
6 oz parsnip, finely diced
6 oz celeriac, finely diced
3 celery stalks, sliced thinly crosswise
4 tomatoes, peeled, quartered and deseeded
4 oz button or closed-cup mushrooms, thinly sliced
3-inch length English cucumber, diced
7-oz can water chestnuts or bamboo shoots, drained and sliced
15 oz can bean-sprouts or palm hearts, rinsed, drained and sliced
4 scallions, trimmed and thinly sliced
1 garlic clove, crushed
2 tbsp sunflower oil

*SWEET & SOUR SAUCE:*
2 tbsp wine vinegar
2 tbsp clear honey
1 tbsp tomato paste
2 tbsp soy sauce
2 tbsp sherry
1–2 tsp sweet chili sauce (optional)
2 tsp cornstarch

STEP 2

**1** Prepare the selected vegetables, cutting them into uniform lengths.

**2** Combine the sauce ingredients in a bowl, blending together well.

**3** Heat the oil in the wok, swirling it around until really hot. Add the scallions and garlic and stir-fry for 1 minute.

STEP 4

**4** Add the prepared vegetables – the harder and firmer ones first – and stir-fry for 2 minutes. Then add the softer ones such as mushrooms, snow peas and tomatoes and continue to stir-fry for 2 minutes.

**5** Add the sweet and sour mixture to the wok and bring to a boil quickly, tossing all the vegetables until they are thoroughly coated and the sauce has thickened. Serve hot.

STEP 5

# CHAPTER FOUR

# *Light Dishes*

Here's a selection of recipes that fit the bill for everyday light meals or simple snacks. They use interesting combinations of fresh fruit, salad ingredients and vegetables, and are all very quick and easy to prepare.

The Quesadillas on page 66 and the Burritos on page 62 are both made with wheat or corn tortillas, and are popular snack foods in Mexico, where the recipes originate. These are ideal for hectic modern lives, as they can be served hot or cold, with a knife and fork or simply eaten with fingers as a filling snack on the run. They are also handy for packing in lunch boxes for any young vegetarians in the family.

If you are looking for ideas for a light meal to serve friends, try the Pear & Roquefort Salad on page 58 or the Cauliflower Roulade on page 64. They are sophisticated, taste great and are easy to make.

Opposite: *Fresh salad ingredients and herbs add plenty of flavor and variety to a light meal.*

# VEGETABLE MEDLEY

*Serve this crisp and colorful vegetarian dish with pitta bread, chapattis or naan bread.*

STEP 1

**SERVES 4**

5 oz young, tender green beans
8 baby carrots
6 baby turnips
½ small cauliflower
2 tbsp vegetable oil
2 large onions, sliced
2 garlic cloves, chopped finely
1¼ cups natural yogurt
1 tbsp cornstarch
2 tbsp tomato paste
large pinch chili powder
salt

**1** Top and tail the beans and snap them in half. Cut the carrots in half and the turnips in quarters. Divide the cauliflower into florets, discarding the thickest part of the stalk. Steam the vegetables over boiling, salted water for 3 minutes, then turn them into a colander and plunge them at once in a large bowl of cold water to prevent further cooking.

**2** Heat the oil in a pan and fry the onions until they are translucent. Stir in the garlic and cook for 1 further minute.

**3** Mix together the yogurt, cornstarch and tomato paste to form a smooth paste. Stir this paste into the onions in the pan and cook for 1–2 minutes until the sauce is well blended.

**4** Drain the vegetables well, then gradually stir them into the sauce, taking care not to break them up. Season with salt and chili powder to taste, cover and simmer gently for 5 minutes, until the vegetables are just tender. Taste and adjust the seasoning if necessary. Serve immediately.

STEP 1

STEP 3

## PITTAS

You can serve this lightly spiced vegetable dish as a filling for pitta breads. To do this, thicken the sauce slightly by simmering it, uncovered, before adding the partly cooked vegetables.

STEP 4

STEP 1

STEP 3

STEP 4

STEP 5

# PEAR & ROQUEFORT SALAD

*The sweetness of the pear makes it a perfect partner for radiccio, which is sharp, and arugula which is peppery. The Roquefort dressing completes this wonderful marriage.*

SERVES 4

*2 oz Roquefort cheese*
*²/₃ cup natural yogurt*
*milk (optional)*
*2 tbsp chopped chives*
*few lollo rosso leaves*
*few radiccio leaves*
*arugula leaves*
*2 ripe pears*
*pepper*
*chopped chives, to garnish*

**1** Mash the cheese with a fork and blend in the yogurt gradually until smooth, adding a little milk if necessary. Add the chives with pepper to taste.

**2** Break the lollo rosso into manageable pieces. Arrange on individual plates with the radiccio and arugula leaves.

**3** Quarter and core the pears, and cut into slices.

**4** Arrange some pear slices over the salad on each plate.

**5** Drizzle the dressing over the top and garnish with chives.

## LETTUCE

If you buy lettuce that is not pre-washed, prepare it carefully. Break off and discard the outer leaves and any damaged leaves. Rinse the lettuce carefully and either pat dry with paper towels, or spin in a salad spinner, or wrap loosely in a dish cloth, gather up the loose ends and swing it around – simple, but effective! It is best to do this outside, as some water will leak through the cloth.

## ROQUEFORT CHEESE

A blue cheese from the southern Massif Central in France, Roquefort is creamy-white with blue-green veins running through it, and has a strong flavor.

If you prefer, you can cut the Roquefort cheese into cubes and add it to the salad greens with the pears and pour a herb vinaigrette over the salad.

STEP 1

STEP 1

STEP 2

STEP 3

# MAQUE CHOUX

*This classic corn dish was introduced to the Cajuns of Louisiana by the local Native Americans. It is stepped up in flavor with traditional Cajun ingredients: onion, bell pepper, tomato and Tabasco sauce.*

SERVES 4–6

1 large tomato
15 g/¹/₂ oz/ 1 tbsp butter or margarine
¹/₂ onion, chopped
1 small green bell pepper, cored, deseeded
    and chopped
generous 4 cups corn kernels, defrosted
    if frozen
¹/₂ tsp salt
¹/₂ tsp Tabasco sauce

**1** Skin, seed and chop the tomato. Melt the butter or margarine in a large heavy-based skillet. Add the onion and bell pepper and cook for 5 minutes until tender.

**2** Stir in the corn, tomato, salt and Tabasco, stirring well.

**3** Reduce the heat to a gentle simmer and cook the mixture for 10–15 minutes or until the corn is tender.

**4** Serve hot with rice and pasta dishes.

### FRESH CORN

Fresh corn kernels undoubtedly make the best Maque Choux. To remove the kernels from fresh cobs, pull away the leaves and all the silks clinging to the corn, then trim the stems level with the base of the cobs. Stand each cob upright, pointed end uppermost, then slice away the kernels with a sharp knife as close to the cob as possible. Fresh corn kernels can be frozen for up to 12 months for convenience.

**STEP 1**

**STEP 2**

**STEP 4**

**STEP 5**

# BURRITOS

*A filling of scrambled eggs, together with a spicy pumpkin seed, herb and yogurt mixture and sliced tomatoes, is rolled into either wheat or corn tortillas.*

SERVES 4

2 oz pumpkin seeds, toasted
3–4 scallions, trimmed and sliced
1 chilli, deseeded and finely chopped
4 tbsp chopped fresh parsley
1 tbsp chopped fresh cilantro
6 tbsp natural yogurt
salt and pepper
4 wheat or corn tortillas (see page 18)
2 tbsp butter
4 tbsp milk
1 garlic clove, crushed
6 eggs
4 oz peeled chopped tomatoes (optional)
2 tomatoes, peeled and sliced

*TO GARNISH:*
*shredded lettuce*
*1 quantity Tomato Salsa (see page 30)*

**1** Toast the pumpkin seeds lightly under a moderate broiler or in a heavy-based skillet, without adding any fat, then chop finely. Put into a food processor with the scallions and chili and work until well blended.

**2** Add the chopped parsley and cilantro, followed by the yogurt, and blend until well mixed. Season to taste.

**3** Wrap the tortillas in foil and warm through in a preheated oven at 350°F for a few minutes.

**4** Melt the butter in a pan with the milk, garlic and seasoning. Remove from the heat and beat in the eggs. Cook over a gentle heat, stirring, until just scrambled. Stir in the tomatoes, if using.

**5** Lay out the tortillas. Spoon the scrambled egg down the center of each and top with the pumpkin seed mixture followed by the sliced tomatoes.

**6** Roll up the tortillas and serve as they are, garnished with the shredded lettuce and tomato salsa.

### MICROWAVE HINT

If preferred, the burritos may be reheated before serving for 1 minute in a microwave oven set on Full Power.

STEP 3

STEP 4

STEP 6

STEP 7

# CAULIFLOWER ROULADE

*A light-as-air mixture of eggs and vegetables produces a stylish vegetarian dish that can be enjoyed hot or cold.*

SERVES 6

1 small cauliflower, divided into florets
4 eggs, separated
³/4 cup Cheddar cheese, grated
¹/4 cup cottage cheese
large pinch grated nutmeg
¹/2 tsp mustard powder
salt and pepper

*FILLING:*
1 bunch watercress, trimmed
¹/4 cup butter
¹/4 cup all-purpose flour
³/4 cup natural yogurt
¹/4 cup Cheddar cheese, grated
¹/4 cup cottage cheese

**1** Line a jelly roll pan with baking parchment.

**2** Steam the cauliflower until just tender. Drain and run cold water on it to prevent further cooking. Place the cauliflower in a food processor and chop finely.

**3** Beat the egg yolks, then stir in the cauliflower, ¹/2 cup of the Cheddar cheese and the cottage cheese. Season with salt, nutmeg, mustard and pepper. Whisk the egg whites until stiff but not

dry, then fold into the cauliflower mixture, using a metal spoon.

**4** Spread the mixture evenly in the prepared pan and bake in a preheated oven at 400°F for 20–25 minutes until well risen and golden brown.

**5** Finely chop the watercress, reserving a few sprigs to garnish. Melt the butter in a small pan and add the watercress. Cook for 3 minutes, stirring, until it has collapsed. Blend in the flour, then stir in the yogurt and simmer for 2 minutes. Stir in the cheeses.

**6** Turn out the roulade on to a damp dish cloth covered with baking parchment. Peel off the parchment and leave 1 minute for the steam to escape. Roll up the roulade, including a new sheet of parchment, starting from one narrow end.

**7** Unroll the roulade, spread the filling to within 1 inch of the edges, and roll up tightly. Transfer to a cookie sheet), sprinkle on the remaining Cheddar cheese and return to the oven for 5 minutes. Serve hot or cold.

STEP 1

STEP 3

STEP 3

STEP 4

# QUESADILLAS

*These are an ideal vegetarian dish. A 'lightly hot' flavoring is given to the mixture of cheeses, scallions and cilantro that makes up the filling for these folded tortillas, which are baked.*

SERVES 4

*8 corn or wheat tortillas (see page 18)*

*FILLING:*
*6 oz Feta cheese or white Cheshire cheese*
*6 oz Mozzarella cheese*
*6 tbsp grated Parmesan cheese*
*6 scallions, trimmed and chopped*
*1–2 garlic cloves, crushed*
*1 tbsp sweet chili sauce*
*1 tbsp chopped fresh cilantro*
*1 cooked potato, grated coarsely*
*salt and pepper*
*beaten egg or egg white*
*oil for brushing*

*TO SERVE:*
*shredded lettuce*
*1 quantity Tomato Salsa (see page 30)*

**1** To make the filling, grate the Feta and Mozzarella coarsely into a bowl and mix in the Parmesan cheese, scallions, garlic, sweet chili sauce, cilantro, grated potato and seasoning.

**2** If the tortillas are too firm to bend in half, dip each one into a pan of gently simmering water until just soft and drain on paper towels.

**3** Place about 1½ tbsp of the cheese filling on one side of each tortilla and fold in half. Brush the edges with beaten egg or egg white.

**4** Fold over and press the edges together well. Place the quesadillas on lightly greased cookie sheets and brush each one with a little oil. Cook in a preheated oven at 375°F for 12–15 minutes or until they are lightly browned.

**5** Serve the quesadillas either hot or warm with shredded lettuce and tomato salsa as accompaniments.

### ALTERNATIVE FILLINGS

This cheese filling makes Quesadillas an excellent dish for vegetarians, but the filling can equally well be based on fish or meat instead for non-vegetarian members of the family. Eggs are another tasty choice for vegetarians.

# CHAPTER FIVE

# Desserts

End your meal with one of the delicious desserts – there is a recipe in this chapter certain to please everyone. They also have the advantage for busy cooks that most can be made ahead.

When planning a menu, select a dessert that complements the dishes that are served before it. If you serve a very spicy meal, for example, consider the soothing Cinnamon Baked Custard on page 70 or Nectarines in Almond Liqueur on page 74. If your meal has a Mexican theme, the unusual bread pudding on page 73 will make a perfect ending. It is flavored with orange rind and raisins, and baked in a tortilla case. Alternatively, serve the Sweet Tortilla Fritters on page 80. In the summer, when fresh fruit is abundant and at its peak, few desserts could be more delicious than the fruit salad recipe on page 78. The recipe suggests serving it with fromage frais or cream, but it would also be delicious with the cinnamon-flavored ice cream on page 76.

*Opposite: Flavourful fresh fruit is always welcomed as an almost-instant dessert. Choose a selection of seasonal fruit for interesting flavour combinations.*

STEP 1

STEP 2

STEP 3

STEP 4

# CINNAMON BAKED CUSTARD

*This dish, similar to the more familiar crème caramel, is made either in individual pots or in one large container to be turned out before eating. Serve plain or with cream.*

**SERVES 6**

*³/₄ cup superfine sugar*
*3 tbsp water*

*CUSTARD:*
*5 eggs*
*3 tbsp superfine sugar*
*2¹/₂ cups milk*
*3 tbsp heavy cream*
*few drops vanilla flavoring (extract)*
*good pinch ground allspice*
*¹/₂ tsp ground cinnamon*
*pouring or whipped cream, to serve*
  *(optional)*

**1** Prepare a 6–7-inch deep round cake pan, or 6 individual ramekin dishes or dariole moulds by rinsing with cold water. Put the sugar into a heavy-based saucepan with the water and mix together. Heat gently, stirring constantly until the sugar has dissolved. Bring to a boil, increase the heat and boil uncovered and without further stirring, until the sugar turns a golden brown.

**2** Pour the caramel quickly into the large container or divide between the individual ones, tipping so the caramel evenly coats the base and a little way up the sides of the container(s). Leave for a few minutes to set.

**3** To make the custard, whisk the eggs together lightly with the sugar. Whisk in the milk and cream and strain into a jug. Whisk the vanilla, allspice and cinnamon into the custard and pour over the caramel.

**4** Place the container(s) in a baking pan and add boiling water to come half-way up the sides of the container(s). Lay a sheet of greased greaseproof paper or foil over the custard.

**5** Place in a preheated oven at 300°F, allowing about 45 minutes for the individual custards or 1–1¹/₄ hours for the large one, cooking until set and until a knife inserted in the custard comes out clean. Remove from the water bath and let cool, then chill thoroughly.

**6** Dip each container briefly in hot water, leave to rest for a minute or so, then shake gently to loosen and invert on to a serving dish or individual plates, allowing the caramel to flow around the custard. Serve plain or with pouring or whipped cream.

# MEXICAN BREAD PUDDING

*This is somewhat different from the traditional bread pudding, though it still contains raisins, nuts, orange rind and spices, together with toasted French bread soaked in a syrup, and a layer of sharp cheese. The whole mixture is encased and baked in tortillas.*

STEP 3

SERVES 6

1 small French stick loaf
4 tbsp butter

*SYRUP:*
$^{3}/_{4}$ cup soft brown sugar
scant 1 cup water
1 cinnamon stick
6 whole cloves or pinch ground cloves
$^{1}/_{4}$ tsp apple pie spice
$1^{1}/_{4}$ cups milk
3–4 wheat or corn tortillas, each
    7–8 inches (see page 18)
1 cup raisins
$^{3}/_{4}$ cup almonds, flaked or chopped
grated rind of 1 orange
$2^{1}/_{2}$ oz sharp Cheddar cheese, grated

**1** Cut the bread into ½-in slices (about 14). Spread each side with some of the butter. Place on a cookie sheet and toast in a preheated oven at 350°F until golden brown, about 10 minutes.

**2** Meanwhile, make the syrup: put the sugar and water into a pan with the cinnamon stick, cloves and apple pie spice. Heat gently until dissolved and then simmer for 2 minutes. Strain into a jug, discarding the spices, and mix in the milk.

**3** Use the remaining butter to grease a 7½ cup ovenproof dish. Use the tortillas to line the dish, cutting them to fit neatly.

**4** Dip half the baked bread slices into the syrup and lay over the tortillas.

**5** Combine the raisins, almonds and orange rind and sprinkle half over the bread, followed by half the cheese.

**6** Dip the remaining bread in the syrup and lay over the raisin mixture, then sprinkle with the remaining raisins, almonds, orange rind and cheese.

**7** Pour the remaining syrup into the dish, and place in a preheated oven at 400°F for 20 minutes. Reduce the temperature to 325°F, cover with a sheet of greaseproof paper or foil and continue to cook for about 30 minutes. Serve hot, warm, or cold cut into wedges, with cream, ice cream or natural yogurt.

STEP 4

STEP 5

STEP 6

# NECTARINES IN ALMOND LIQUEUR CREAM

*Nectarines, figs and strawberries are broiled with a rich liqueur-flavored cream to give a crusted sugary finish.*

STEP 1

STEP 2

STEP 3

STEP 4

**SERVES 4**

2 nectarines or peaches
1½ cups strawberries
2 figs
⅔ cup heavy cream
2 tbsp almond-flavored liqueur such as
   Amaretto di Saronno
3 tbsp brown crystal sugar

**1** Halve and pit the nectarines, then slice them.

**2** Hull and halve the strawberries, cut each fig into 8 wedges and arrange on 4 flameproof plates with the strawberries and nectarines.

**3** Whip the cream and liqueur together until the cream just holds its shape. Spoon over the fruit on each plate.

**4** Sprinkle the sugar generously over the cream.

**5** Place each plate under a preheated hot broiler until bubbling and golden. Serve immediately.

### TIPS

Bananas make a good alternative if you cannot get figs. Slice them into thick, diagonal slices and toss them in lemon juice to prevent them from browning.

To make the broiling easier, you can arrange the fruit on one large platter and cover it with the liqueur-flavored cream and sugar. This means that you will only have to broil once, and no one is left waiting for their dessert. Each person can then serve themselves from the central plate.

Make sure the sugar becomes a dark brown, almost burned, as this crispness adds a great texture and flavor to the fruit.

STEP 1

STEP 2

STEP 3

STEP 4

# VANILLA & CINNAMON ICE CREAM

*This rich creamy ice cream flavored with vanilla and cinnamon has an added tang from the addition of crème fraîche; chopped toasted nuts can be added. Serve with fresh fruits or a chocolate sauce.*

SERVES 4–6

*4 eggs*
*¼ cup superfine sugar*
*scant 2 cups milk*
*few drops vanilla extract*
*1 tsp ground cinnamon*
*scant 1 cup crème fraîche or*
*    1¼ cups heavy cream*
*3 tbsp toasted chopped hazelnuts*
*    or almonds (optional)*
*fresh fruits, to decorate*

**1** To make the custard, whisk the eggs with the sugar until thick in a heatproof bowl. Heat the milk to just below boiling point and whisk into the egg mixture gradually.

**2** Stand the bowl over a pan of gently simmering water and cook slowly, stirring almost constantly until thickened sufficiently to coat the back of a spoon quite thickly. Remove from the heat and stir in the vanilla extract and cinnamon. Cover with plastic wrap and leave until cold.

**3** If using crème fraîche, just mix evenly through the custard; or if using heavy cream, whip until thick but not too stiff and fold into the custard.

Cover the bowl or pour into a loaf pan and freeze until just firm.

**4** Remove the ice cream from the freezer and whisk until smooth, turning into a bowl if necessary. This breaks down the ice crystals in the ice cream. Beat in the nuts, if using.

**5** Cover, return to the freezer and freeze until firm. (An ice cream maker may be used if available.)

**6** Serve the ice cream spooned into bowls and decorated with fresh fruits such as strawberries, raspberries, mangoes or guavas, or topped with a chocolate sauce.

## CHOCOLATE SAUCE

To make the chocolate sauce, melt 4 oz dark chocolate with 2 tbsp butter in a bowl and beat in ½ cup of evaporated milk and a few drops of vanilla extract until smooth, heating a little if necessary to remove any lumps. You can add 1–2 tbsp brandy or rum if you like.

STEP 2

STEP 4

STEP 5

STEP 6

# SUMMER FRUIT SALAD

*A mixture of soft summer fruits in an orange-flavored syrup with a dash of port. Serve with fromage frais or whipped cream.*

SERVES 6

$^1/_3$ *cup superfine sugar*
$^1/_3$ *cup water*
*grated rind and juice of 1 small orange*
*2 cups redcurrants, stripped from
    their stalks*
*2 tsp arrowroot*
*2 tbsp port*
*1 cup blackberries*
*1 cup blueberries*
$^3/_4$ *cup strawberries*
*1$^1/_2$ cups raspberries*

**1** Put the sugar, water and grated orange rind into a pan and heat gently, stirring until the sugar has dissolved.

**2** Add the redcurrants and orange juice, bring to a boil and simmer gently for 2–3 minutes.

**3** Strain the fruit, reserving the syrup, and put into a bowl.

**4** Blend the arrowroot with a little water. Return the syrup to the pan, add the arrowroot and bring to the boil, stirring until thickened.

**5** Add the port and mix together well. Then pour over the redcurrants in the bowl.

**6** Add the blackberries, blueberries, strawberries and raspberries. Mix together and let cool.

**7** Serve in individual glass dishes with natural fromage frais or cream.

## USING FROZEN FRUIT

Although this salad is really best made with fresh fruits in season, you can achieve an acceptable result with frozen equivalents, with perhaps the exception of strawberries. You can buy frozen fruits of the forest in most supermarkets, which would be ideal.

STEP 1

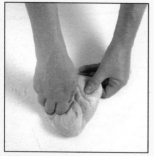

STEP 3

STEP 4

STEP 5

# SWEET TORTILLA FRITTERS

*Sweet tortillas are cut into triangles to be fried and are served dipped in cinnamon sugar as teatime treats, or with fresh fruits and cream or yogurt for a dessert.*

SERVES 4–6

*2 eggs
3 tbsp superfine sugar
1 cup all-purpose flour
³/₄ cup self-raising flour
pinch salt
¹/₄ tsp ground cinnamon
oil for shallow frying*

*CINNAMON SUGAR:
¹/₃ cup superfine sugar
¹/₂ tsp ground cinnamon
good pinch ground ginger*

*TO DECORATE:
clear honey (optional)
mixed fresh fruits*

**1** Put the eggs and sugar into a bowl and whisk together until very thick and pale in color, with the whisk leaving a distinct trail. It is best to use an electric hand mixer.

**2** Sift the 2 flours together with the salt and ground cinnamon. Whisk half of the flour gradually into the egg mixture, then work in the remainder to make a dough.

**3** Turn the dough out on a lightly floured counter and knead until smooth and no longer sticky. (This may be done in a large electric mixer fitted with a dough hook.) Wrap in plastic wrap and leave to rest for about 30 minutes.

**4** Divide the dough into 6 pieces and roll each into a thin circle of about 8 inches, then cut each circle into quarters.

**5** Heat about 1 inch of oil in a skillet until a cube of bread will brown in about 1 minute. Fry the fritters, a few at a time, for about 1 minute on each side, until golden brown and bubbly. Drain on paper towels and toss quickly in a mixture of the sugar, cinnamon and ginger.

**6** Serve the fritters (hot or cold) on a plate, and, if liked, drizzle a little clear honey over them. Decorate with fresh fruits such as sliced mango, figs, passionfruit, nectarines, strawberries, guavas, pomegranates and so on.

**DIPS, NIBBLES & CANAPES**

•

**APPETIZERS & SOUPS**

•

**MAIN COURSES**

•

**VEGETABLE
ACCOMPANIMENTS**

•

**SALADS**

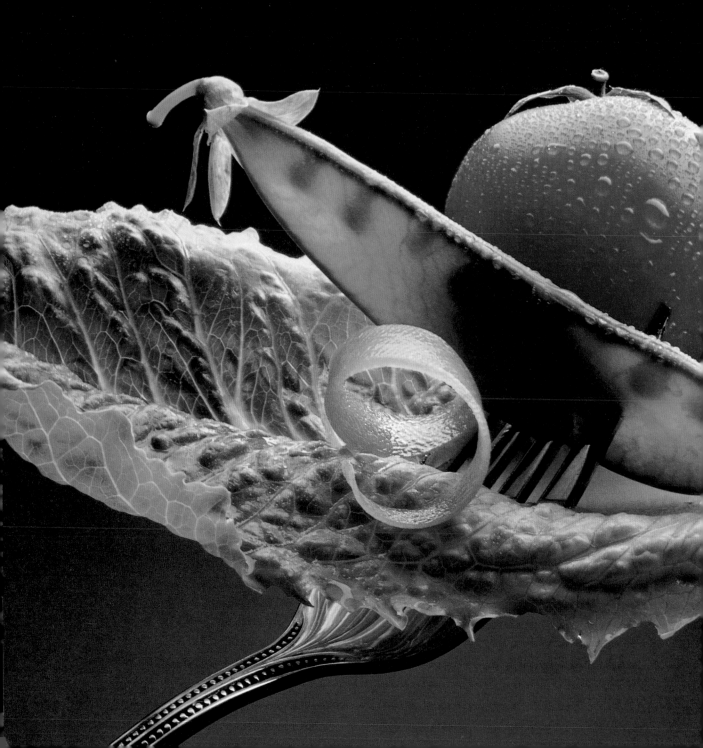

# CHAPTER SIX

# *Dips, Nibbles & Canapés*

Tempt your family or guests with a taste of things to come with these delicious ideas for vegetarian dips, nibbles and canapés – perfect for parties, buffets and for serving with pre-dinner drinks. These bite-sized nibbles make great snacks too – just the thing to have to hand when inviting a few friends around for a drink.

All the recipes are quick and simple to prepare, yet they taste really good – and they are just that little bit different from run-of-the-mill offerings. For example, the Crispy-fried Vegetables with Hot & Sweet Dipping Sauce are a delicious combination of crunchy deep-fried vegetables served with a spicy side dish. Or try Tofu & Vegetable Mini-Kebabs, served with a tasty cashew nut sauce.

Presentation is very important when serving these starters. Dips can look very appetizing served in hollowed-out vegetables, such as green, red or yellow bell peppers and green or red cabbage. Make lots of fresh vegetable crudités for variety, crunch and color (leftovers can always be used in soups or salads). Just before serving, garnish with fresh herbs to give them a "fresh from the garden" look, which adds an attractive finishing flourish.

Opposite: *Bite-sized food makes a tempting prelude to any meal.*

**STEP 1**

**STEP 2**

**STEP 3**

**STEP 4**

# FIERY SALSA WITH TORTILLA CHIPS

*Make this Mexican-style salsa to perk up jaded palates. Its lively flavors really get the tastebuds going!*

SERVES 6

*2 small red chilies*
*1 tbsp lime or lemon juice*
*2 large ripe avocados*
*2-inch piece English cucumber*
*2 tomatoes, peeled*
*1 small garlic clove, crushed*
*few drops Tabasco sauce*
*salt and pepper*
*lime or lemon slices, to garnish*
*tortilla chips, to serve*

**1** Remove and discard the stem and seeds from 1 chili. Chop very finely and place in a mixing bowl. To make a chili 'flower' for garnishing, slice the remaining chili from the stem to the tip several times without removing the stem. Place in a bowl of cold water, so that the "petals" open out.

**2** Add the lime or lemon juice to the mixing bowl. Halve, deseed and peel the avocados. Add to the mixing bowl and mash with a fork. (The lime or lemon juice prevents the avocado from turning brown.)

**3** Chop the cucumber and tomatoes finely and add to the avocado mixture with the crushed garlic.

**4** Season the dip to taste with Tabasco sauce, salt and pepper.

**5** Transfer the dip to a serving bowl. Garnish with slices of lime or lemon and the chili flower. Put the bowl on a large plate, surround with tortilla chips and serve.

## CHILIES

If you're not keen on hot, spicy flavors, make a milder version by omitting the chilies and Tabasco sauce. Take care when handling fresh chilies, as they can irritate the skin. Prepare them quickly and wash your hands afterward. Be careful to avoid touching your eyes during preparation.

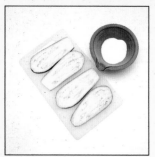

STEP 1

STEP 2

STEP 3

STEP 4

# BAKED EGGPLANT, BASIL & MOZZARELLA ROLLS

*Thin slices of eggplant are fried in olive oil and garlic, and then topped with pesto sauce and finely sliced Mozzarella cheese.*

SERVES 4

2 eggplants, thinly sliced lengthwise
5 tbsp olive oil
1 garlic clove, crushed
4 tbsp pesto sauce
1 1/2 cups Mozzarella cheese, grated
a few basil leaves, torn into pieces
salt and pepper
fresh basil leaves, to garnish

**1** Spread out the slices of eggplant on a counter. Sprinkle liberally with salt and leave for 10–15 minutes to extract the bitter juices. Turn the slices over and repeat. Rinse well with cold water and drain on paper towels.

**2** Heat the olive oil in a large skillet and add the garlic. Fry the eggplant slices lightly on both sides, a few at a time. Drain them on paper towels.

**3** Spread the pesto sauce on to one side of the eggplant slices. Top with the grated Mozzarella cheese and sprinkle with the torn basil leaves. Season with a little salt and pepper. Roll up the slices and secure with wooden toothpicks.

**4** Arrange the aubergine (eggplant) rolls in a greased ovenproof baking dish. Bake in a preheated oven at 350°F for 8–10 minutes.

**5** Transfer the rolls to a warmed serving plate. Scatter with fresh basil leaves and serve at once.

### GRATED CHEESE

If you wish, buy ready-grated cheese from your supermarket or delicatessen, as it can be quite tricky to grate it yourself. Otherwise, you may find it easier to slice the Mozzarella thinly.

STEP 1

STEP 2

STEP 3

STEP 4

# CRISPY-FRIED VEGETABLES WITH HOT & SWEET DIPPING SAUCE

*A Thai-style dipping sauce makes the perfect accompaniment to fresh vegetables in season coated in a light batter and deep-fried.*

**SERVES 4**

*vegetable oil for deep-frying*
*1 lb selection of vegetables, such as*
*cauliflower, broccoli, mushrooms,*
*zucchini, bell peppers and baby corn, cut*
*into even-sized pieces*

*BATTER:*
*1 cup all-purpose flour*
*¹/₂ tsp salt*
*1 tsp superfine sugar*
*1 tsp baking powder*
*3 tbsp vegetable oil*
*scant 1 cup warm water*

*SAUCE:*
*6 tbsp light malt vinegar*
*2 tbsp Thai fish sauce or light soy sauce*
*2 tbsp water*
*1 tbsp soft brown sugar*
*pinch salt*
*2 garlic cloves, crushed*
*2 tsp grated fresh gingerroot*
*2 red chilies, deseeded and finely chopped*
*2 tbsp chopped fresh cilantro*

**1** To make the batter, sift the flour, salt, sugar and baking powder into a large bowl. Add the oil and most of the water. Whisk together to make a smooth batter, adding extra water to give it the consistency of light cream. Chill for 20–30 minutes.

**2** Meanwhile, make the sauce. Heat the vinegar, fish sauce or soy sauce, water, sugar and salt until boiling. Remove from the heat and let cool.

**3** Mix together the garlic, ginger, chilies and cilantro in a small serving bowl. Add the cooled vinegar mixture and stir together.

**4** Heat the vegetable oil for deep-frying in a wok or deep-fat fryer. Dip the prepared vegetables in the batter and fry them, a few at a time, for about 2 minutes until crisp and golden. Drain on paper towels.

**5** Serve the vegetables accompanied by the dipping sauce.

### CILANTRO

Fresh cilantro is a wonderful herb, with a pungent, distinctive flavor. You can use the stem and root as well as the leaves – just make sure that they are thoroughly cleaned before use.

# MINT & CANNELLINI BEAN DIP

*This dip is ideal for pre-dinner drinks or for handing around at a party, accompanied by potato crisps and colorful vegetable crudités. For speed and convenience you could use canned beans if preferred, but remember to double the quantity.*

STEP 2

SERVES 6

1 cup dried cannellini beans
1 small garlic clove, crushed
1 bunch scallions, roughly chopped
handful fresh mint leaves
2 tbsp tahini (sesame seed paste)
2 tbsp olive oil
1 tsp ground cumin
1 tsp ground coriander
lemon juice
salt and pepper
sprigs of fresh mint, to garnish
fresh vegetable crudités, such as cauliflower
    florets, carrots, English cucumber,
    radishes and bell peppers

**1** Soak the cannellini beans overnight in plenty of cold water.

**2** Rinse and drain the beans, put them into a large saucepan and cover them with cold water. Bring to a boil and boil rapidly for 10 minutes. Reduce the heat, cover and simmer for 1 1/2–2 hours until tender.

**3** Drain the beans and transfer them to a bowl or food processor. Add the garlic, scallions, mint, tahini and olive oil.

**4** Blend the mixture for about 15 seconds, or mash well by hand, until smooth.

**5** Transfer the mixture to a bowl and season with ground cumin, ground coriander, lemon juice, salt and pepper, according to taste. Mix well, cover and leave in a cool place for 30 minutes to allow the flavors to develop.

**6** Spoon the dip into serving bowls, garnish with sprigs of fresh mint and surround with the vegetable crudités.

STEP 3

STEP 4

### CANNED BEANS

If using canned cannellini beans, use two 14-oz cans. Drain and rinse well. Add to the bowl or food processor at step 3. Garbanzo beans may be used as an alternative.

STEP 5

STEP 1

STEP 2

STEP 4

STEP 5

# TOFU & VEGETABLE MINI-KEBABS

*Cubes of smoked tofu are speared on satay sticks with crisp vegetables, basted with lemon juice and olive oil, and then broiled. The sauce can be drizzled over the kebabs or served as a dip.*

SERVES 6

10 oz smoked tofu, cut into cubes
1 large red and 1 large yellow bell pepper,
    deseeded and cut into small squares
6 oz button mushrooms, wiped
1 small zucchini, sliced
finely grated rind and juice
    of 1 lemon
3 tbsp olive oil
1 tbsp chopped fresh parsley
1 tsp superfine sugar
salt and pepper
parsley sprigs, to garnish

SAUCE:
1 cup cashew nuts
1 tbsp butter
1 garlic clove, crushed
1 shallot, finely chopped
1 tsp ground coriander
1 tsp ground cumin
1 tbsp superfine sugar
1 tbsp shredded coconut
$^2/_3$ cup natural yogurt

**1** Thread the tofu cubes, bell peppers, mushrooms and zucchini on to bamboo satay sticks. Arrange them in a shallow dish.

**2** Mix together the lemon rind and juice, oil, parsley and sugar. Season well with salt and pepper. Pour over the kebabs, and brush them with the mixture. Leave for 10 minutes.

**3** To make the sauce, scatter the cashew nuts on to a cookie sheet and toast them until lightly browned.

**4** Melt the butter in a saucepan and cook the garlic and shallot gently until softened. Transfer to a blender or food processor and add the nuts, coriander, cumin, sugar, coconut and yogurt. Blend for about 15 seconds. Alternatively, chop the nuts finely and mix with the remaining ingredients.

**5** Place the tofu kebabs under a preheated broiler and cook, turning and basting with the lemon juice mixture, until lightly browned. Garnish with sprigs of parsley, and serve with the cashew nut sauce.

STEP 1

STEP 2

STEP 3

STEP 4

# HERB, TOASTED NUT & PAPRIKA CHEESE NIBBLES

*These tiny cheese balls are rolled in fresh herbs, toasted nuts or paprika to make tasty nibbles for parties, buffets, or pre-dinner drinks.*

SERVES 4

4 oz Ricotta cheese
4 oz brick cheese, finely grated
2 tsp chopped fresh parsley
1/2 cup chopped mixed nuts
3 tbsp chopped fresh herbs, such as parsley,
  chives, marjoram, lovage and chervil
2 tbsp mild paprika
pepper
fresh herb sprigs, to garnish

**1** Mix together the Ricotta and brick cheeses. Add the parsley and pepper and work together until combined.

**2** Form the mixture into small balls. Cover and chill for about 20 minutes to firm.

**3** Scatter the chopped nuts on to a cookie sheet and place them under a preheated broiler until lightly browned. Take care as they can easily burn. Let cool.

**4** Sprinkle the nuts, herbs and paprika into 3 separate small bowls. Divide the cheese balls into 3 piles and roll 1 quantity in the nuts, 1 quantity in the herbs and 1 quantity in the paprika.

**5** Arrange on a serving platter. Chill until ready to serve, and then garnish with sprigs of fresh herbs.

## CHEESE AND NUTS

You can buy small bags of chopped mixed nuts at most supermarkets. Alternatively, buy whole, blanched nuts and chop them finely in a food processor or blender.

To ring the changes, use soft cheese instead of Ricotta, and sharp Cheddar or Red Leicester instead of the brick cheese.

# CHAPTER SEVEN

# Starters & Soups

With so many fresh ingredients readily available, it is very easy to create some deliciously different starters and soups to make the perfect introduction to a vegetarian meal. The ideas in this chapter are an inspiration to cook and a treat to eat, and they give an edge to the appetite that makes the main course even more enjoyable.

When choosing a appetizer, make sure that you provide a good balance of flavors, colors and textures that offer variety and contrast. Decide whether you want to serve a hot or a cold appetizer – generally it is a good idea to begin with a hot course if the main one is cold, and vice versa. Balance the nature of the recipes too – a rich main course would be best if preceded by a light appetizer, just sufficient to interest the palate and stimulate the tastebuds.

Give some consideration to the amount of food you are likely to serve: you could easily overwhelm appetites by serving portions that are too large, especially if you plan to make a dessert too. The recipes in this section will give an impressive start to a special meal, especially if you can spend a little extra time arranging and garnishing the food attractively. Then these delicious recipes will look as good as they taste.

Opposite: *Choose from a wide range of fresh ingredients, and your soups and starters will be rich in both color and flavor.*

STEP 1

STEP 2

STEP 3

STEP 5

# PLUM TOMATO SOUP

*Homemade tomato soup is easy to make and always tastes better than bought varieties. Try this version with its Mediterranean influences – plum tomatoes, red onions and fresh Italian herbs. Serve it with warm Italian bread topped with olive and hazelnut spread.*

### SERVES 4

*2 tbsp olive oil*
*2 red onions, chopped*
*2 celery stalks, chopped*
*1 carrot, chopped*
*1 lb fresh plum tomatoes, halved*
*3 cups vegetable stock*
*1 tbsp chopped fresh oregano, or 1 tsp*
*   dried oregano*
*1 tbsp chopped fresh basil, or 1 tsp*
*   dried basil*
*²/₃ cup dry white wine*
*2 tsp superfine sugar*
*1 cup hazelnuts, toasted*
*1 cup black or green olives*
*handful fresh basil leaves*
*1 tbsp olive oil*
*1 loaf Italian-style bread*
*salt and pepper*
*sprigs of fresh basil, to garnish*

**1** Heat the olive oil in a large saucepan and fry the chopped onions, celery and carrot gently until softened.

**2** Add the tomatoes, stock, chopped herbs, wine and sugar. Bring to a boil, then cover and simmer gently for about 20 minutes.

**3** Place the toasted hazelnuts in a blender or food processor with the olives and basil leaves and process until combined, but not too smooth. Alternatively, chop the nuts, olives and basil leaves finely and pound in a mortar and pestle, then turn into a small bowl. Add the olive oil, process or beat thoroughly for a few seconds, and then turn the mixture into a serving bowl.

**4** Warm the Italian bread in a preheated oven at 375°F for 3–4 minutes.

**5** Blend the soup in a blender or a food processor, or press through a strainer until smooth. Check the seasoning, adding salt and pepper according to taste. Ladle into 4 warmed soup bowls. Garnish with sprigs of basil. Slice the bread and spread with the olive and hazelnut paste. Serve with the soup.

### TOMATOES

If you wish, remove the skins from the tomatoes with a fork while they are still in the pan. If you cannot buy fresh plum tomatoes, use ordinary tomatoes or a 14-oz can of plum tomatoes instead.

STEP 1

STEP 2

STEP 4

STEP 5

# SPINACH & MASCARPONE SOUP WITH CARAWAY SEED CROUTONS

*Spinach is the basis for this delicious soup, which has Mascarpone cheese stirred through it to give it a creamy texture and flavor. Try sorrel or watercress instead of spinach for a pleasant change.*

SERVES 4

¼ cup butter
1 bunch scallions, trimmed and chopped
2 celery stalks, chopped
3 cups spinach or sorrel, or
   3 bunches watercress
3½ cups vegetable stock
1 cup Mascarpone cheese
1 tbsp olive oil
2 slices thick-cut bread, cut into cubes
½ tsp caraway seeds
salt and pepper
sesame bread sticks, to serve

**1** Melt half the butter in a very large saucepan. Add the scallions and celery, and cook slowly for about 5 minutes, until softened.

**2** Pack the spinach, sorrel or watercress into the saucepan. Add the stock and bring to a boil, then reduce the heat and simmer, covered, for 15–20 minutes.

**3** Transfer the soup to a blender or food processor and blend until smooth, or rub through a strainer. Return to the saucepan.

**4** Add the Mascarpone cheese to the soup and heat gently, stirring, until smooth and blended. Taste and season with salt and pepper.

**5** Heat the remaining butter with the oil in a skillet. Add the bread cubes and fry in the hot fat until golden brown, adding the caraway seeds towards the end of cooking, so that they do not burn.

**6** Ladle the soup into 4 warmed bowls. Sprinkle with the caraway-flavored croûtons and serve at once, accompanied by the sesame bread sticks.

### VARIATIONS

Any leafy vegetable can be used to make this soup to give variations to the flavor. For anyone who grows their own vegetables, it is the perfect recipe for experimenting with a glut of produce. Try young beet leaves or surplus lettuces for a change.

# CHEESE, GARLIC & HERB PATE

*This wonderful soft cheese pâté is fragrant with the aroma of fresh herbs and garlic. Pile it on to small plates, garnish with salad and serve with crisp triangles of Melba toast to make the perfect appetizer.*

STEP 1

SERVES 4

1 tbsp butter
1 garlic clove, crushed
3 scallions, chopped finely
2 tbsp chopped mixed fresh herbs, such as parsley, chives, marjoram, oregano and basil
½ cup cream cheese
1½ cups sharp Cheddar cheese, finely grated
pepper
4–6 slices of white bread from a medium-cut sliced loaf
mixed salad leaves and cherry tomatoes, to serve

TO GARNISH:
ground paprika
fresh herb sprigs

**1** Melt the butter in a small skillet and fry the garlic and scallions together gently for 3–4 minutes until softened. Let cool.

**2** Put the cream cheese in a large mixing bowl and beat until soft. Add the garlic and scallions. Stir in the herbs, mixing well.

STEP 2

**3** Add the Cheddar cheese and work the mixture together to form a stiff paste. Cover and chill until ready to serve.

**4** To make the Melba toast, toast the slices of bread on both sides, and then cut off the crusts. Using a sharp bread knife, cut through the slices horizontally to make very thin slices. Cut into triangles and then broil the untoasted sides lightly.

**5** Arrange the mixed salad leaves on 4 serving plates with the cherry tomatoes. Pile the cheese pâté on top and sprinkle with a little paprika. Garnish with sprigs of fresh herbs and serve with the Melba toast.

STEP 3

### CHEESE

You can vary this recipe by choosing different cheeses – try Italian Ricotta in place of the cream cheese or substitute brick or Red Leicester cheese for the Cheddar. Do make sure that the hard cheese is very finely grated for best results.

STEP 4

STEP 2

STEP 3

STEP 5

STEP 6

# LEEK & SUN-DRIED TOMATO TIMBALES

*Angel-hair pasta, known as cappellini, is mixed with fried leeks, sun-dried tomatoes, fresh oregano and beaten eggs, and baked in ramekins.*

**SERVES 4**

3 oz angel-hair pasta (cappellini)
2 tbsp butter
1 tbsp olive oil
1 large leek, finely sliced
$\frac{1}{2}$ cup sun-dried tomatoes in oil, drained and chopped
1 tbsp chopped fresh oregano or 1 tsp dried oregano
2 eggs, beaten
generous $\frac{1}{3}$ cup light cream
1 tbsp grated Parmesan cheese
salt and pepper
lettuce leaves, to serve

*SAUCE:*
1 small onion, finely chopped
1 small garlic clove, crushed
12 oz tomatoes, peeled and chopped
1 tsp mixed dried Italian herbs
4 tbsp dry white wine

**1** Cook the pasta in plenty of boiling, lightly salted water for about 3 minutes until just tender. Drain and rinse with cold water to cool quickly.

**2** Meanwhile, heat the butter and oil in a skillet. Fry the leek gently until softened and cooked, about 5–6 minutes. Add the sun-dried tomatoes and oregano, and cook for a further 2 minutes. Remove from the heat.

**3** Add the leek mixture to the pasta. Stir in the beaten eggs, cream and Parmesan cheese. Season with salt and pepper. Divide between 4 greased ramekin dishes or dariole moulds.

**4** Place the dishes in a roasting pan with enough warm water to come halfway up their sides. Bake in a preheated oven at 350°F for about 30 minutes until set.

**5** To make the tomato sauce, fry the onion and garlic in the remaining butter and oil until softened. Add the tomatoes, herbs and wine. Cover and cook slowly for about 20 minutes until pulpy. Blend in a food processor until smooth, or press through a strainer.

**6** Turn out the timbales on to 4 warmed serving plates. Pour over a little sauce and garnish with sprigs of oregano. Serve with the lettuce leaves.

# AVOCADO CREAM TERRINE

*The smooth, rich taste of ripe avocados combines well with thick, creamy yogurt and light cream to make this impressive terrine.*

**STEP 1**

**STEP 2**

**STEP 3**

**STEP 4**

SERVES 6

4 tbsp cold water
2 tsp gelozone (vegetarian
   gelatine)
1 tbsp lemon juice
4 tbsp mayonnaise
²/₃ cup thick natural yogurt
²/₃ cup light cream
2 ripe avocados
salt and pepper
mixed salad greens, to serve

*TO GARNISH:*
*English cucumber slices*
*nasturtium flowers*

**1** Assemble the water, gelozone, lemon juice, mayonnaise, yogurt and cream. Peel the avocados and remove the seeds. Place all these ingredients in a blender or food processor, or a large bowl.

**2** Process for 10–15 seconds, or beat by hand, until smooth.

**3** Transfer the mixture to a small saucepan and heat gently, stirring constantly, until just boiling.

**4** Pour the mixture into a 3³/₄ cup plastic food storage box or terrine. Let cool and set, and then refrigerate for 1¹/₂–2 hours until chilled.

**5** Turn the mixture out of its container and cut into neat slices. Arrange a bed of salad greens on 6 serving plates. Place a slice of avocado terrine on top and garnish with cucumber slices and nasturtium flowers.

### AVOCADOS

Avocados soon turn brown, so it is important to mix them with the lemon juice as soon as they are peeled and mashed to prevent this from happening.

STEP 1

STEP 2

STEP 3

STEP 5

# BUTTER-CRUST TARTLETS WITH FETA CHEESE

*These crispy-baked bread cases, filled with sliced tomatoes, Feta cheese, black olives and quail's eggs, are quick to make and taste delicious.*

SERVES 4

8 slices of bread from a medium-cut
    large loaf
$1/2$ cup butter, melted
4 oz Feta cheese, cut into small cubes
4 cherry tomatoes, cut into wedges
8 pitted black or green olives, halved
8 quail's eggs, hard-cooked
2 tbsp olive oil
1 tbsp wine vinegar
1 tsp wholegrain mustard
pinch of superfine sugar
salt and pepper
parsley sprigs, to garnish

**1** Remove the crusts from the slices of bread. Trim the bread into squares and flatten each piece with a rolling pin.

**2** Brush the pieces of bread with melted butter, and then arrange them in bun or muffin pans. Press a piece of crumpled foil into each bread case to secure in place. Bake in a preheated oven at 375°F for about 10 minutes or until crisp and browned.

**3** Meanwhile, mix together the Feta cheese, tomatoes and olives. Shell the eggs and quarter them. Mix together

the olive oil, vinegar, mustard and sugar. Season with salt and pepper.

**4** Remove the bread cases from the oven and discard the foil. Let cool.

**5** Just before serving, fill the cooked bread cases with the cheese and tomato mixture. Arrange the eggs on top and spoon over the dressing. Garnish with sprigs of parsley.

## BITE-SIZE

For canapés and nibbles, the bread can be cut into smaller pieces and used to line mini muffin pans. They can then be filled with mixtures of your choice. (Try using the Cheese, Garlic & Herb Pâté on page 105.)

# CHAPTER EIGHT

# *Main Courses*

Anyone who ever thought that vegetarian meals were dull
will be proved wrong by the rich variety of dishes in this
chapter. In these recipes, you will recognize influences from Indian,
Italian, Greek and Indonesian cooking, and although you may not
have used some of the ingredients often, you should have no
difficulty in buying them locally. With luck you will discover a
whole range of new ingredients that can easily be added to your
shopping list and used to great effect in any number of dishes,
both new and old. The Indonesian Chestnut & Vegetable Stir-Fry on
page 124, for example, may introduce you to sesame oil for the first
time. It is fragrant and flavorsome and adds a new dimension
of subtlety that, once tried, you will want to use all the time
in your stir-fries.

While each recipe may encourage you to try new ingredients,
don't be afraid to substitute some of your own favorites
where appropriate. For instance, you may prefer to make the
Almond & Sesame Nut Roast on page 122 with peanuts instead
of almonds, for a more economical everyday occasion. There
is no reason why you can't experiment and enjoy adding your
own signature to these imaginative ideas.

Opposite: *Select the freshest basic ingredients that you can find to be sure of an unforgettable dinner party dish.*

STEP 1

STEP 2

STEP 3

STEP 4

# TAGLIATELLE TRICOLORE WITH BROCCOLI & BLUE CHEESE SAUCE

*Some of the simplest and most satisfying dishes are made with pasta. This delicious combination of tagliatelle with its Gorgonzola and Mascarpone cheese sauce is one of them.*

SERVES 4

*10 oz tagliatelle tricolore (plain, spinach- and tomato-flavoured noodles)*
*8 oz broccoli, broken into small florets*
*1½ cups Mascarpone cheese*
*1 cup chopped Gorgonzola cheese,*
*1 tbsp chopped fresh oregano*
*2 tbsp butter*
*salt and pepper*
*fresh oregano sprigs, to garnish*
*grated Parmesan cheese, to serve*

**1** Cook the tagliatelle in plenty of boiling, lightly salted water until just tender, according to the instructions on the package. The Italians call this *al dente*, which means "to the tooth."

**2** Meanwhile, cook the broccoli florets in a small amount of lightly salted, boiling water. Avoid overcooking the broccoli, so that it retains its color and texture.

**3** Heat the Mascarpone and Gorgonzola cheeses together gently in a large saucepan until they are melted. Stir in the oregano and season with salt and pepper.

**4** Drain the pasta thoroughly. Return it to the cheese sauce and add the butter, tossing the tagliatelle to coat it. Drain the broccoli well and add to the pasta with the sauce, tossing gently to mix.

**5** Divide the pasta between 4 warmed serving plates. Garnish with sprigs of fresh oregano and serve with Parmesan cheese.

ALTERNATIVES

Choose your favourite pasta shapes to use in this recipe as an alternative to tagliatelle. If you prefer, substitute a creamy blue Stilton for the Gorgonzola.

STEP 1

STEP 2

STEP 3

STEP 4

# MUSHROOM & PINE NUT TARTS

*These mushroom-filled filo pastry tarts make a delicious main course meal. Different varieties of mushroom are becoming more widely available in supermarkets, so use this recipe to make the most of them.*

SERVES 4

*1 lb frozen filo pastry, thawed*
*½ cup butter, melted*
*1 tbsp hazelnut oil*
*1 oz pine nuts*
*12 oz mixed mushrooms, such as buttons, chestnut, oyster and shiitake*
*2 tsp chopped fresh parsley*
*8 oz soft goat's cheese*
*salt and pepper*
*parsley sprigs, to garnish*
*lettuce, tomatoes, English cucumber and scallions, to serve*

**1** Cut the sheets of filo pastry into pieces about 4 inches square and use them to line 4 individual tart pans, brushing each layer of pastry with melted butter. Line the pans with foil or baking parchment and baking beans. Bake in a preheated oven at 400°F for 6–8 minutes or until light golden brown. Remove the tarts from the oven and take out the foil or parchment and beans carefully. Reduce the oven temperature to 350°F.

**2** Put any remaining butter into a large saucepan with the hazelnut oil and fry the pine nuts gently until golden brown. Lift them out with a

perforated spoon and drain them on paper towels.

**3** Add the mushrooms to the saucepan and cook them gently, stirring frequently, for 4–5 minutes. Add the chopped parsley and season to taste with salt and pepper.

**4** Spoon an equal amount of goat's cheese into the base of each cooked filo tart. Divide the mushrooms between them and scatter the pine nut over the top.

**5** Return the tarts to the oven for 5 minutes to heat through, and then serve them, garnished with sprigs of parsley. Serve with lettuce, tomatoes, cucumber andscallions.

### FILO PASTRY

Filo pastry is easy to use, but handle it carefully as it is quite delicate. As you use the pastry, keep it covered with plastic wrap or a damp cloth to prevent it from drying out.

STEP 1

STEP 2

STEP 3

STEP 4

# RICOTTA & SPINACH PACKAGES

*Ricotta cheese and spinach make a great flavor combination, especially when encased in light puff-pastry parcels. Gently fried onions and green peppercorns add to the success of this dish.*

SERVES 4

3 cups spinach, trimmed and washed
   thoroughly
2 tbsp butter
1 small onion, finely chopped
1 tsp green peppercorns
1 lb puff pastry
1 cup Ricotta cheese
1 egg, beaten
salt
fresh herb sprigs, to garnish
fresh vegetables, to serve

**1** Pack the spinach into a large saucepan. Add a little salt and a very small amount of water and cook until wilted. Drain well and let cool. Then squeeze out any excess moisture with the back of a spoon. Chop roughly.

**2** Melt the butter in a small saucepan and fry the onion gently until softened, but not browned. Add the green peppercorns and cook for 2 more minutes. Remove from the heat, add the spinach and mix together.

**3** Roll out the puff pastry thinly on a lightly floured counter and cut into 4 squares, each 7 inches across. Place a quarter of the spinach mixture in the center of each square and top with a quarter of the cheese.

**4** Brush a little beaten egg around the edges of the pastry squares and bring the corners together to form packages. Press the edges together firmly to seal. Lift the packages onto a greased cookie sheet, brush with beaten egg and bake in a preheated oven at 400°F for 20–25 minutes until risen and golden brown.

**5** Serve hot, garnished with sprigs of fresh herbs and accompanied by fresh vegetables.

### GARNISHING

Any pastry trimmings can be rolled out and cut into leaves to garnish the packages. Brush with beaten egg to glaze.

Fresh green peppercorns can be bought in small jars, preserved in brine. They have a milder flavor than black peppercorns and are ideal when used whole or lightly crushed in a variety of savory recipes.

**STEP 1**

# INDIAN CURRY FEAST

*This vegetable curry is quick and easy to prepare, and it tastes superb.*
*If you make a colorful Indian salad to accompany it and a cool mint*
*raita to refresh the palate, you have the makings of a real feast!*

**STEP 2**

**SERVES 4**

1 tbsp vegetable oil
2 garlic cloves, crushed
1 onion, chopped
3 celery stalks, sliced
1 apple, chopped
1 tbsp medium-strength curry powder
1 tsp ground ginger
4 oz thin green beans, sliced
8 oz cauliflower, broken into florets
8 oz potatoes, cut into cubes
2 cups mushrooms, wiped and sliced
13-oz can garbanzo beans, drained
2½ cups vegetable stock
1 tbsp tomato paste
1 oz golden raisins
sant 1 cup basmati rice
1 tbsp garam masala

**SALAD:**
4 tomatoes, chopped
1 green chili, deseeded and finely chopped
3-inch piece English cucumber, chopped
1 tbsp fresh cilantro
4 scallions, trimmed and chopped

**MINT RAITA:**
²/₃ cup natural yogurt
1 tbsp chopped fresh mint
fresh mint sprigs, to garnish

**1** Heat the oil in a large saucepan and fry the garlic, onion, celery and apple gently for 3–4 minutes. Add the curry powder and ginger, and cook gently for 1 more minute.

**2** Add the remaining ingredients except the rice and garam masala. Bring to a boil, then reduce the heat. Cover and simmer for 35–40 minutes.

**3** To make the salad, combine all the ingredients. Cover and chill.

**4** To make the raita, mix the yogurt and mint together. Transfer to a serving dish, then cover and chill.

**5** Cook the rice in boiling, lightly salted water until just tender, according to the instructions on the pachage. Drain thoroughly.

**6** Just before serving, stir the garam masala into the curry. Divide between 4 warmed serving plates, and serve with the salad, mint raita and rice. Garnish the raita with fresh mint.

**STEP 4**

**STEP 6**

**STEP 1**

**STEP 2**

**STEP 3**

**STEP 4**

# ALMOND & SESAME NUT ROAST

*Toasted almonds are combined with sesame seeds, rice and vegetables in this tasty vegetarian roast. Serve it with a delicious onion and mushroom sauce to reap the compliments.*

SERVES 4

2 tbsp sesame or olive oil
1 small onion, finely chopped
$^1/_4$ cup risotto rice
$1^1/_4$ cups vegetable stock
1 large carrot, grated
1 large leek, trimmed and finely chopped
2 tsp sesame seeds, toasted
$^3/_4$ cup chopped almonds, toasted
$^1/_2$ cup ground almonds
$^3/_4$ cup grated sharp Cheddar cheese,
2 eggs, beaten
1 tsp dried mixed herbs
salt and pepper
Italian parsley sprigs, to garnish
fresh vegetables, to serve

SAUCE:
2 tbsp butter
1 small onion, chopped finely
$1^1/_4$ cup mushrooms, chopped finely
$^1/_4$ cup all-purpose flour
$1^1/_4$ cups vegetable stock

**1** Heat the oil in a large skillet and fry the onion gently for 2–3 minutes. Add the rice and cook slowly for 5–6 minutes, stirring frequently.

**2** Add the vegetable stock, bring to a boil and then simmer for about 15 minutes, or until the rice is tender. Add a little extra water if necessary. Remove from the heat and transfer to a large mixing bowl.

**3** Add the carrot, leek, sesame seeds, almonds, cheese, eggs and herbs to the mixture. Mix well and season with salt and pepper. Transfer the mixture to a greased 1 lb loaf pan, levelling the surface. Bake in a preheated oven at 350°F for about 1 hour, until set and firm. Leave in the pan for 10 minutes.

**4** To make the sauce, melt the butter in a small saucepan and fry the onion until dark golden brown. Add the mushrooms and cook for a further 2 minutes. Stir in the flour, cook slowly for 1 minute and then gradually add the stock. Bring to the boil, stirring constantly, until thickened and blended. Season to taste.

**5** Turn out the nut roast, slice and serve on warmed plates with fresh vegetables, accompanied by the sauce. Garnish with sprigs of Italian parsley.

**STEP 1**

**STEP 2**

**STEP 3**

**STEP 4**

# INDONESIAN CHESTNUT & VEGETABLE STIR-FRY

*This colorful, spicy stir-fry, which is served with peanut sauce, has an Indonesian influence, with the shallots, chilies, ginger, fresh cilantro and limes.*

SERVES 4

*SAUCE:*
*1 cup unsalted peanuts, roasted and ground*
*2 tsp hot chili sauce*
*³/₄ cup coconut milk*
*2 tbsp soy sauce*
*1 tbsp ground coriander*
*pinch ground turmeric*
*1 tbsp dark muscovado sugar*

*STIR-FRY:*
*3 tbsp sesame oil*
*3–4 shallots, finely sliced*
*1 garlic clove, sliced finely*
*1–2 red chilies, deseeded and finely chopped*
*1 large carrot, cut into fine strips*
*1 yellow and 1 red bell pepper, deseeded and*
    *cut into fine strips*
*1 zucchini, cut into fine strips*
*4 oz sugar snap peas, trimmed*
*3-inch piece of English cucumber,*
    *cut into strips*
*8 oz oyster mushrooms, wiped and torn into*
    *small pieces, if large*
*8 oz canned whole peeled chestnuts, drained*
*2 tsp grated fresh gingerroot*
*finely grated rind and juice of 1 lime*
*1 tbsp chopped fresh cilantro*
*salt and pepper*
*slices of lime, to garnish*

**1** To make the sauce, put all the ingredients into a small pan. Heat gently and simmer for 3–4 minutes.

**2** Heat the sesame oil in a wok or large skillet. Add the shallots, garlic and chilies and stir-fry for 2 minutes.

**3** Add the carrot, bell peppers, zucchini and sugar snap peas to the wok or skillet and stir-fry for 2 more minutes.

**4** Add all the remaining ingredients to the wok or skillet and stir-fry briskly for about 5 minutes, or until the vegetables are crisp, yet crunchy.

**5** Divide the stir-fry between 4 warmed serving plates, and garnish with slices of lime. Serve with the peanut sauce.

# CHAPTER NINE

# Vegetable Accompaniments

If you are running short of ideas for interesting ways to serve vegetables with your meals, these recipes will be a welcome inspiration. There is now such an abundance of fresh vegetables available all year round that there is no excuse not to serve interesting accompaniments. It is true that some produce may seem too expensive if out of season or imported from abroad, but you can always cook locally grown vegetables in unusual ways to give them a totally new treatment. Or just buy unusual varieties on special occasions or in small quantities. When added to other vegetables, they can make the entire dish seem more exotic.

Herbs and spices can be used to great effect with vegetables. For instance, the Stir-Fried Winter Vegetables on page 138 is composed of familiar types of vegetables, brought to life with fresh cilantro, a deliciously fragrant herb that is easily obtainable.

These recipes need not be mere accompaniments; some are delicious enough to serve as main courses in their own right. However you choose to serve them, you won't be disappointed.

*Opposite: The range of vegetables that is now available means endless possibilities for exotic and unusual dishes.*

**STEP 1**

**STEP 2**

**STEP 3**

**STEP 5**

# BELL PEPPERS WITH ROSEMARY BASTE

*The flavor of broiled or roasted bell peppers is very different from when they are eaten raw, so try them cooked this way. They taste even better when brushed with a crushed rosemary baste as they cook.*

SERVES 4

*4 tbsp olive oil*
*finely grated rind of 1 lemon*
*4 tbsp lemon juice*
*1 tbsp balsamic vinegar*
*1 tbsp crushed fresh rosemary, or 1 tsp*
*    dried rosemary*
*2 red bell peppers, halved, cored and deseeded*
*2 yellow bell peppers, halved, cored and*
*    deseeded*
*2 tbsp pine nuts*
*salt and pepper*
*fresh rosemary sprigs, to garnish*

**1** Mix together the olive oil, lemon rind, lemon juice, vinegar and crushed rosemary. Season with salt and pepper.

**2** Place the bell peppers, skin-side uppermost, on the rack of a broiler pan, lined with foil. Brush the lemon juice mixture over them.

**3** Broil the bell peppers until the skin begins to char, basting frequently with the lemon juice mixture. Remove from the heat, cover with foil to trap the steam and leave for 5 minutes.

**4** Meanwhile, scatter the pine nuts on to the broiler rack and toast them lightly.

**5** Peel the bell peppers, slice them into strips and place them in a warmed serving dish. Sprinkle with the pine nuts and drizzle any remaining lemon juice mixture over them. Garnish with sprigs of fresh rosemary and serve at once.

### PEELING BELL PEPPERS

Covering the hot bell peppers with a piece of foil after broiling traps the escaping steam. This loosens their skins, so that they are easy to peel, and it helps to keep them warm.

STEP 1

STEP 2

STEP 3

STEP 4

# CREAMY BAKED FENNEL

*Baked fennel tastes fabulous in this creamy sauce, flavored with caraway seeds. A crunchy bread crumb topping gives an interesting change of texture.*

SERVES 4

*2 tbsp lemon juice*
*2 bulbs fennel, trimmed*
*1/4 cup low-fat soft cheese*
*2/3 cup light cream*
*2/3 cup milk*
*1 egg, beaten*
*1/4 cup butter*
*2 tsp caraway seeds*
*1 cup fresh white bread crumbs*
*salt and pepper*
*fresh parsley sprigs, to garnish*

**1** Bring a large saucepan of water to a boil and add the lemon juice. Slice the bulbs of fennel thinly and add them to the saucepan. Cook for 2–3 minutes to blanch, and then drain them well, and arrange in a buttered ovenproof dish.

**2** Beat the soft cheese in a bowl until smooth. Add the cream, milk and beaten egg, and whisk together until combined. Season with salt and pepper and pour over the fennel.

**3** Melt 1 tablespoon of the butter in a small skillet and fry the caraway seeds gently for 1–2 minutes to release their flavor and aroma. Sprinkle over the fennel.

**4** Melt the remaining butter in a skillet. Add the bread crumbs and fry gently until lightly browned. Sprinkle evenly over the surface of the fennel.

**5** Bake in a preheated oven at 350°F and bake for 25–30 minutes or until the fennel is tender.

**6** Serve, garnished with sprigs of parsley.

### ALTERNATIVE

If you cannot find any fennel in the shops, leeks make a delicious alternative. Use about 1½ lb, making sure that they are washed thoroughly to remove all traces of soil.

STEP 1

STEP 2

STEP 3

STEP 4

# ZUCCHINI, CARROT & FETA CHEESE PATTIES

*Grated carrots, zucchini and Feta cheese are combined with cumin seeds, poppy seeds, curry powder and chopped parsley to make these delicious patties, which are fried gently until golden brown.*

SERVES 4

2 large carrots
1 large zucchini
1 small onion
2 oz Feta cheese
$1/4$ cup all-purpose flour
$1/2$ tsp cumin seeds
$1/2$ tsp poppy seeds
1 tsp medium curry powder
1 tbsp chopped fresh parsley
1 egg, beaten
2 tbsp butter
2 tbsp vegetable oil
salt and pepper
fresh herb sprigs, to garnish

**1** Grate the carrots, zucchini, onion and Feta cheese coarsely, either by hand or in a food processor.

**2** Mix together the flour, cumin seeds, poppy seeds, curry powder and parsley in a large bowl. Season well with salt and pepper.

**3** Add the carrot mixture to the seasoned flour, tossing well to combine. Stir in the beaten egg and mix well.

**4** Heat the butter and oil in a large skillet. Place heaped tablespoonfuls of the carrot mixture in the pan, flattening them slightly with the back of the spoon. Fry gently for about 2 minutes on each side, until crisp and golden brown. Drain on paper towels and keep warm until all the mixture is used.

**5** Serve, garnished with sprigs of fresh herbs.

## VARIATION

If you want to vary the flavor of these patties, omit the cumin seeds and curry powder and substitute 1 tbsp chopped fresh oregano for the parsley.

# SAUTE OF SUMMER VEGETABLES WITH TARRAGON DRESSING

*The freshness of lightly cooked summer vegetables is enhanced by the aromatic flavor of the tarragon and white wine dressing, which is poured over the hot vegetables just before serving.*

**SERVES 4**

8 oz baby carrots, scrubbed
4 oz green beans
2 zucchini, trimmed
1 bunch large scallions, trimmed
1 bunch radishes, trimmed
1/4 cup butter
2 tbsp light olive oil
2 tbsp white wine vinegar
4 tbsp dry white wine
1 tsp superfine sugar
1 tbsp chopped fresh tarragon
salt and pepper
fresh tarragon sprigs, to garnish

**1** Trim and halve the carrots, slice the beans and zucchini and halve the scallions and radishes, so that all the vegetables are cut to even-sized pieces.

**2** Melt the butter in a large skillet or wok. Add all the vegetables and fry them over a medium heat, stirring frequently.

**3** Heat the olive oil, vinegar, white wine and sugar in a small saucepan. Remove from the heat and add the tarragon.

**4** When the vegetables are just cooked, but still retain their crunchiness, pour over the "dressing." Stir through, and then transfer to a warmed serving dish. Garnish with sprigs of fresh tarragon and serve at once.

## ALTERNATIVES

Use any combination of fresh vegetables for this dish, but remember to serve them while still slightly crunchy for the best texture and flavor. The vegetables also retain more of their nutrients when cooked this way.

If you cannot find any fresh tarragon, substitute a different herb such as basil, oregano or chives.

STEP 1

STEP 2

STEP 3

STEP 4

STEP 1

STEP 3

STEP 4

STEP 5

# SPICY STUFFED CHINESE LEAVES

*Mushrooms, scallions, celery and rice are flavored with five-spice powder and wrapped in Chinese leaves in this tasty vegetable dish. If you want to serve it as a main course, simply double the quantities.*

SERVES 4

8 large Chinese leaves
¹/₃ cup long-grain rice
¹/₂ vegetable bouillon cube
¹/₄ cup butter
1 bunch scallions, trimmed and finely
   chopped
1 celery stalk, finley chopped
1¹/₄ cups button mushrooms, sliced
1 tsp five-spice powder
1¹/₄ cups strained tomatoes
salt and pepper
fresh chives, to garnish

**1** Blanch the Chinese leaves in boiling water for 1 minute. Refresh them under cold running water and drain well. Be careful not to tear them.

**2** Cook the rice in plenty of boiling water, flavored with the bouillon cube, until just tender. Drain well.

**3** Meanwhile, melt the butter in a skillet and fry the scallions and celery gently for 3–4 minutes until softened, but not browned. Add the mushrooms and cook for a further 3–4 minutes, stirring frequently.

**4** Add the cooked rice to the pan with the five-spice powder. Season with salt and pepper and stir well to combine the ingredients.

**5** Lay out the Chinese leaves on a counter and divide the rice mixture between them. Roll each leaf into a neat package to enclose the stuffing. Place them, seam-side down, in a greased ovenproof dish. Pour the strained tomatoes over them and cover with foil.

**6** Bake in a preheated oven at 375°F for 25–30 minutes. Serve immediately, garnished with chives.

### CABBAGE LEAVES

Cabbage leaves, either from a hard white variety or from a more leafy spring cabbage, can be used instead of Chinese leaves. Take care when removing the leaves and blanching them, to prevent them from tearing.

STEP 1

STEP 2

STEP 3

STEP 4

# STIR-FRIED WINTER VEGETABLES WITH CILANTRO

*Ordinary winter vegetables are given extraordinary treatment in this lively stir-fry, just the thing for perking up jaded palates.*

SERVES 4

*3 tbsp sesame oil*
*¼ cup blanched almonds*
*1 large carrot, cut into thin strips*
*1 large turnip, cut into thin strips*
*1 onion, finely sliced*
*1 garlic clove, crushed*
*3 celery stalks, finley sliced*
*4 oz Brussels sprouts, trimmed and halved*
*4 oz cauliflower, broken into florets*
*2 cups white cabbage, shredded*
*2 tsp sesame seeds*
*1 tsp grated fresh gingerroot*
*½ tsp medium chili powder*
*1 tbsp chopped fresh cilantro*
*1 tbsp light soy sauce*
*salt and pepper*
*fresh cilantro sprigs, to garnish*

**1** Heat the sesame oil in a wok or large skillet. Stir-fry the almonds until lightly browned, then lift them out and drain on paper towels.

**2** Add all the vegetables to the wok or skillet, except for the cabbage. Stir-fry briskly for 3–4 minutes.

**3** Add the cabbage, sesame seeds, ginger and chili powder to the vegetables. Cook, stirring, for 2 minutes.

**4** Add the chopped cilantro, soy sauce and almonds to the mixture, stirring them through gently. Serve the vegetables, garnished with sprigs of fresh cilantro.

### SESAME OIL

Sesame oil is not essential for making this stir-fry, but it does give an excellent flavor and is a typical ingredient of oriental cookery, though it is generally used for sprinkling over food or flavoring sauces. Vegetable or olive oil could be used instead, or groundnut or corn oil, which are frequently used in Chinese cooking.

Substitute different winter vegetables, to make a change. Try leeks, parsnips, rutabaga, salsify, celeriac or red cabbage as alternatives.

# CHAPTER TEN

# *Salads*

With the range of fresh produce that is now widely available, dull or lifeless salads should be a thing of the past. In this selection you will discover a number of bright ideas bursting with flavor and colour. Make one of these salads to accompany your main meal, or make larger portions to serve alone. You could also select a recipe from this chapter to serve as an appetizer.

Some of these recipes are light and fruity, others are more substantial. Choose the right salad to serve with your main course choice to offer a good balance – make sure that the flavors and textures complement rather than clash with one another. Alternatively, make a selection of these salads to serve at parties and buffets with lots of crusty new bread, a tempting cheese board and plenty of fresh fruit for an irresistible spread.

Remember that the secret of a successful salad relies on two important aspects: the freshness of the ingredients and the choice of a complementary dressing to bring out their flavors. Choose your salad ingredients carefully, buying them at the peak of perfection. They will then taste superb, especially when combined with one of the unusual dressings suggested here.

*Opposite: Both fruits and vegetables can be used to make delicious and refreshing salads, which will add color, texture and flavor to any meal.*

STEP 1

STEP 2

STEP 3

STEP 4

# MARINATED VEGETABLE SALAD

*Lightly steamed vegetables taste superb served slightly warm in a marinade of olive oil, white wine, vinegar and fresh herbs.*

SERVES 4–6

6 oz baby carrots, trimmed
2 celery hearts, cut into 4 pieces
4 oz sugar snap peas or snow peas
1 bulb fennel, sliced
6 oz small asparagus spears
1½ tbsp sunflower seeds
fresh dill sprigs, to garnish

DRESSING:
4 tbsp olive oil
4 tbsp dry white wine
2 tbsp white wine vinegar
1 tbsp chopped fresh dill
1 tbsp chopped parsley
salt and pepper

**1** Steam the carrots, celery, sugar snap peas or snow peas, fennel and asparagus over gently boiling water until just tender, retaining a little "bite."

**2** Meanwhile, mix together the olive oil, wine, vinegar and chopped herbs. Season well with salt and pepper.

**3** When the vegetables are cooked, transfer them to a serving dish and pour over the dressing at once. The hot vegetables will absorb the flavor of the dressing as they cool.

**4** Scatter the sunflower seeds on a cookie sheet and toast them under a preheated broiler until lightly browned. Sprinkle them over the vegetables.

**5** Serve the salad while the vegetables are still slightly warm, garnished with sprigs of fresh dill.

### VARIATION

Sesame seeds or pine nuts can be used instead of sunflower seeds for sprinkling over the vegetables. Keep an eye on them while broiling, as they can burn easily.

STEP 1

STEP 2

STEP 4

STEP 4

# RED ONION, CHERRY TOMATO & PASTA SALAD

*Pasta tastes perfect in this lively salad, dressed with red wine vinegar, lemon juice, basil and olive oil. Sliced red onions, roast bell peppers, zucchini and tomatoes add wonderful flavors and colors.*

SERVES 4

1½ cups pasta shapes
1 yellow bell pepper, halved, cored
    and deseeded
2 small zucchini, sliced
1 red onion, thinly sliced
4 oz cherry tomatoes, halved
a handful fresh basil leaves, torn into
    small pieces
salt and pepper
fresh basil sprigs, to garnish

DRESSING:
4 tbsp olive oil
2 tbsp red wine vinegar
2 tsp lemon juice
1 tsp Dijon mustard
½ tsp superfine sugar
handful of fresh basil leaves, torn into small
    pieces

**1** Cook the pasta in plenty of boiling, lightly salted water for about 8 minutes or until just tender.

**2** Meanwhile, place the bell pepper halves, skin-side uppermost, under a preheated broiler until they just begin to char. Let cool, then peel and slice them into strips.

**3** Cook the zucchini in a small amount of boiling, lightly salted water for 3–4 minutes until cooked, but still crunchy. Drain and refresh under cold running water to cool quickly.

**4** To make the dressing, mix together the olive oil, vinegar, lemon juice, mustard and sugar. Season well with salt and pepper. Add the basil leaves.

**5** Drain the pasta well and tip it into a large serving bowl. Add the dressing and toss well. Add the bell pepper zucchini, onion and cherry tomatoes, stirring to combine. Cover and leave at room temperature for about 30 minutes to allow the flavors to develop.

**6** Serve, garnished with sprigs of fresh basil.

## PASTA SHAPES

Choose pasta shapes that hold the dressing well for this salad. Conchiglie (pasta shells) or torchietti (little torches) are ideal.

STEP 1

STEP 2

STEP 3

STEP 5

# MELON, MANGO & GRAPE SALAD WITH GINGER & HONEY DRESSING

*A little freshly grated gingerroot mixed with thick, creamy yogurt and clear honey makes a perfect dressing for this refreshing melon salad.*

SERVES 4

1 cantaloup melon
1/2 cup black grapes, halved and pipped
1/2 cup green grapes
1 large mango
1 bunch watercress, trimmed
iceberg lettuce leaves, shredded
2 tbsp olive oil
1 tbsp cider vinegar
1 passionfruit
salt and pepper

DRESSING:
2/3 cup thick, natural full-fat yogurt
1 tbsp clear honey
1 tsp grated fresh gingerroot

**1** To make the dressing for the melon, mix together the yogurt, honey and ginger.

**2** Halve the melon and scoop out the seeds. Slice, peel and cut into chunks. Mix with the grapes.

**3** Slice the mango on each side of its large flat pit. On each mango half, slash the flesh into a criss-cross pattern down to, but not through, the skin. Push the skin from underneath to turn the mango halves inside out.

Now remove the flesh and add to the melon mixture.

**4** Arrange the watercress and lettuce on 4 serving plates. Make the dressing for the salad greens by mixing together the olive oil and cider vinegar with a little salt and pepper. Drizzle over the watercress and lettuce.

**5** Divide the melon mixture between the 4 plates and spoon over the yogurt dressing. Scoop the seeds out of the passionfruit and sprinkle them over the salads.

### GINGER

Grated fresh gingerroot gives a great flavor to this recipe, but if you can't get it, substitute 1/2 teaspoon of ground ginger instead.

146

# THREE-BEAN SALAD

*Fresh thin green beans are combined with canned soy beans and red kidney beans in a chive and tomato dressing, to make a quick, tasty and nutritious salad.*

STEP 1

SERVES 4–6

3 tbsp olive oil
1 tbsp lemon juice
1 tbsp tomato paste
1 tbsp light malt vinegar
1 tbsp chopped fresh chives
6 oz thin green beans
14-oz can soy beans, rinsed and drained
14-oz can red kidney beans, rinsed
 and drained
2 tomatoes, chopped
4 scallions, trimmed and chopped
4 oz Feta cheese, cut into cubes
salt and pepper
mixed salad greens, to serve
chopped fresh chives, to garnish

**1** Put the olive oil, lemon juice, tomato paste, vinegar and chives into a large bowl and whisk together until thoroughly combined.

**2** Cook the thin green beans in a little boiling, lightly salted water for 4–5 minutes until just cooked. Drain, refresh under cold running water and drain again.

**3** Add the green beans, soy beans and red kidney beans to the dressing, stirring to mix together.

**4** Add the tomatoes, scallions and Feta cheese to the bean mixture, tossing gently to coat in the dressing. Season well with salt and pepper.

**5** Arrange the mixed salad leaves on 4 serving plates. Pile the bean salad on to the plates and garnish with chopped chives.

STEP 2

STEP 3

## BEANS

You can substitute different types of canned beans for the soy beans and red kidney beans. Try navy beans, black-eyed peas or garbanzo beans instead.

STEP 4

STEP 1

STEP 2

STEP 3

STEP 4

# MOROCCAN ORANGE & COUS-COUS SALAD

*Cous-cous is wonderful in salads as it readily takes up the flavor of the dressing. It is a semolina-based food made from durum wheat, and it simply has to be soaked to swell the grains before use.*

SERVES 4–6

2 cups cous-cous
1 bunch scallions, trimmed and finely
    chopped
1 small green bell pepper, deseeded
    and chopped
4-inch piece English cucumber, chopped
6-oz can garbanzo beans, rinsed and drained
$1/_3$ cup golden raisins or raisins
2 oranges
salt and pepper
lettuce leaves, to serve
fresh mint sprigs, to garnish

DRESSING:
finely grated rind of 1 orange
1 tbsp chopped fresh mint
$2/_3$ cup natural yogurt

**1** Put the cous-cous into a bowl and cover with boiling water. Let soak for about 15 minutes to swell the grains, then stir with a fork to separate them.

**2** Add the scallions, green bell pepper, English cucumber, garbanzo beans and golden raisins or raisins to the cous-cous, stirring to combine. Season well with salt and pepper.

**3** To make the dressing, mix together the orange rind, mint and yogurt. Pour over the cous-cous mixture and stir well.

**4** Using a sharp serrated knife, remove the peel and pith from the oranges. Cut them into segments, removing all the membrane.

**5** Arrange the lettuce leaves on 4 serving plates. Divide the cous-cous mixture between the plates and arrange the orange segments on top. Garnish with sprigs of fresh mint and serve.

### ORANGE JUICE

When preparing the oranges, catch any juice in a bowl so that it can be stirred through the salad.

STEP 2

STEP 3

STEP 4

STEP 5

# PINK GRAPEFRUIT, AVOCADO & DOLCELATTE SALAD

*Fresh pink grapefruit segments, ripe avocados and sliced soft blue cheese make a deliciously different salad combination.*

SERVES 4

*½ romaine lettuce*
*½ oak leaf lettuce*
*2 pink grapefruit*
*2 ripe avocados*
*6 oz soft blue cheese, thinly sliced*
*fresh basil sprigs, to garnish*

*DRESSING:*
*4 tbsp olive oil*
*1 tbsp white wine vinegar*
*salt and pepper*

**1** Arrange the lettuce leaves on 4 serving plates or in a salad bowl.

**2** Remove the peel and pith from the grapefruit with a sharp serrated knife, catching the grapefruit juice in a bowl.

**3** Segment the grapefruit by cutting down each side of the membrane. Remove all the membrane. Arrange the segments on the serving plates.

**4** Peel, pit and slice the avocados, dipping them in the grapefruit juice to prevent them from going brown. Arrange the slices on the salad with the soft blue cheese.

**5** To make the dressing, combine any remaining grapefruit juice with the olive oil and wine vinegar. Season with salt and pepper, mixing well.

**6** Drizzle the dressing over the salads. Garnish with fresh basil leaves and serve at once.

TIPS

Pink grapefruit segments make a very attractive color combination with the avocados, but ordinary grapefruit will work just as well.
To help avocados to ripen, keep them at room temperature in a brown paper bag.

**DIPS, SAUCES & MARINADES**

•

**FILLED THINGS**

•

**MAIN COURSES**

•

**SALADS**

•

**DESSERTS**

# 3

## VEGETARIAN BARBECUES

# CHAPTER ELEVEN

# Dips, Sauces & Marinades

In this chapter, you will find some delicious ideas for tasty dips, a spicy barbecue sauce, rich marinades and lively dressings – those all-important details that complete the barbecue and make the food taste superb. There are some great barbecue basics here, designed to excite the palate and to add to the flavor of the finished food.

One point that is crucial to the whole idea of outdoor eating is that although the food should be simple and easy to prepare, it should still taste wonderful. All the ideas in this chapter have been developed with that aim in mind. Here you will find recipes that are quick to put together, taking only moments to assemble.

When marinating food, it is a good idea to prepare it several hours before the barbecue, so that it has plenty of time to soak up the flavors of the marinade. The same principle applies to the sauces, dips and dressings too, as the longer the ingredients are combined, the more the flavors will develop and mellow. Besides, the earlier these are prepared, the less you will have to do at the barbecue!

Opposite: *A simple dressing made with fresh herbs, spices, aromatic oils, sharp vinegars and a range of fruit and vegetable ingredients will add an invaluable flavor to your barbecued food.*

# BUTTERED NUT & LENTIL DIP

*This tasty dip is very easy to make. It is perfect to have at barbecues, as it gives your guests something to nibble while they are waiting for their cooked food.*

STEP 1

STEP 2

STEP 3

STEP 4

SERVES 4

*¹/₄ cup butter*
*1 small onion, chopped*
*¹/₃ cup red lentils*
*1¹/₄ cups vegetable stock*
*¹/₂ cup blanched almonds*
*¹/₂ cup pine nuts*
*¹/₂ tsp ground coriander*
*¹/₂ tsp ground cumin*
*¹/₂ tsp freshly grated gingerroot*
*1 tsp chopped fresh cilantro*
*salt and pepper*
*fresh cilantro sprigs, to garnish*

*TO SERVE:*
*fresh vegetable crudités*
*bread sticks*

**1** Melt half the butter in a saucepan and fry the onion gently until golden brown.

**2** Add the lentils and vegetable stock. Bring to a boil, then reduce the heat and simmer gently, uncovered, for 25–30 minutes until the lentils are tender. Drain well.

**3** Melt the remaining butter in a small skillet. Add the almonds and pine nuts and fry them gently until golden brown. Remove from the heat.

**4** Put the lentils, almonds and pine nuts, with any remaining butter, into a blender or food processor. Add the ground coriander, cumin, ginger and fresh cilantro. Blend for 15–20 seconds until smoothor push the lentils through a strainer to make a smooth paste. Mix with the finely chopped nuts, spices and herbs.

**5** Season the dip with salt and pepper and garnish with sprigs of fresh cilantro. Serve with fresh vegetable crudités and bread sticks.

## VARIATIONS

Green or brown lentils can be used, but they will take longer to cook than red lentils.

If you wish, substitute peanuts for the almonds to make a more economical version.

Ground ginger can be used instead of fresh gingerroot – substitute ¹/₂ teaspoon and add it to the food processor or blender with the other spices.

STEP 1

STEP 2

STEP 3

STEP 4

# TZATZIKI WITH PITTA BREAD & BLACK OLIVE DIP

*Tzatziki is a Greek dish, made with natural yogurt, mint and English cucumber. It tastes superb with warm pitta bread and the black olive dip provides a delicious contrast of flavor.*

SERVES 4

*½ English cucumber*
*1 cup thick natural yogurt*
*1 tbsp chopped fresh mint*
*salt and pepper*
*4 pitta breads*

*DIP:*
*2 garlic cloves, crushed*
*¾ cup pitted black olives*
*4 tbsp olive oil*
*2 tbsp lemon juice*
*1 tbsp chopped fresh parsley*

*TO GARNISH:*
*fresh mint sprigs*
*fresh parsley sprigs*

**1** To make the tzatziki, peel the cucumber and roughly chop. Sprinkle it with salt and leave it to stand for 15–20 minutes. Rinse with cold water and drain well.

**2** Mix the cucumber, yogurt and mint together. Season with salt and pepper and transfer to a serving bowl. Cover and chill for 20–30 minutes.

**3** To make the dip, put the crushed garlic and olives into a blender or food processor and blend for 15–20 seconds. Alternatively, chop them very finely.

**4** Add the olive oil, lemon juice and parsley to the blender or food processor and blend for a few more seconds. Alternatively, mix with the chopped garlic and olives and mash together. Season with salt and pepper.

**5** Wrap the pitta breads in foil and place over the barbecue for 2–3 minutes, turning once to warm through. Alternatively, heat in the oven or under the broiler. Cut into pieces and serve with the tzatziki and black olive dip, garnished with sprigs of fresh mint and parsley.

## TIPS

Sprinkling the cucumber with salt draws out some of its moisture, making it crisper. If you are in a hurry, you can omit this procedure.

Use green olives instead of black ones if you prefer.

# HEAVENLY GARLIC DIP
# WITH CRUDITES

*Anyone who loves garlic will adore this dip – it is very potent! Keep it
warm over the hot coals to one side of the barbecue, and dip raw
vegetables or chunks of French bread into it.*

STEP 1

SERVES 4

2 bulbs garlic
6 tbsp olive oil
1 small onion, finely chopped
2 tbsp lemon juice
3 tbsp tahini (sesame seed paste)
2 tbsp chopped fresh parsley
salt and pepper

TO SERVE:
fresh vegetable crudités
French bread or warmed pitta breads

**1** Separate the bulbs of garlic into individual cloves. Place them on a baking sheet and roast in a preheated oven at 400°F for 8–10 minutes. Let cool for a few minutes.

**2** Peel the garlic cloves, then chop them finely.

**3** Heat the olive oil in a saucepan or skillet and add the chopped garlic and chopped onion. Fry gently for 8–10 minutes until softened. Remove the pan from the heat.

**4** Mix the lemon juice, tahini and parsley into the garlic mixture. Season to taste with salt and pepper.

Transfer to a small heatproof bowl and keep warm at one side of the barbecue.

**5** Serve with fresh vegetable crudités, chunks of French bread or warm pitta breads.

STEP 2

STEP 3

### SMOKED GARLIC

If you come across smoked garlic, use it in this recipe – it tastes wonderful. There is no need to roast the smoked garlic, so omit the first step.

This dip can also be used to baste kebabs and vegetarian burgers.

STEP 4

163

# TASTY BARBECUE SAUCE

*Just the thing for brushing on to vegetable kebabs and burgers, this sauce takes only minutes to make.*

STEP 1

STEP 2

STEP 3

STEP 4

SERVES 4

2 tbsp butter or margarine
1 garlic clove, crushed
1 onion, finely chopped
1 3-oz can chopped tomatoes
1 tbsp dark muscovado sugar
1 tsp hot chili sauce
1–2 cucmbers (gherkins)
1 tbsp capers, drained
salt and pepper

**1** Melt the butter or margarine in a saucepan and fry the garlic and onion for 8–10 minutes until well browned.

**2** Add the chopped tomatoes, sugar and chili sauce. Bring to the boil, then reduce the heat and simmer gently for 20–25 minutes until thick and pulpy.

**3** Chop the cucumbers and capers finely.

**4** Add the chopped cucumbers and capers to the sauce, stirring well to mix. Cook the sauce for a further 2 minutes.

**5** Taste the sauce and season with a little salt and pepper. Use as a baste for vegetarian kebabs and burgers, or as an accompaniment to other barbecued food.

### TIPS

To make sure that the sauce has a good color, it is important to brown the onions really well to begin with.

When fresh tomatoes are cheap and plentiful, they can be used instead of canned ones. Peel and chop 1 lb, and add them as before.

Substitute chili powder instead of chili sauce, according to taste. If you prefer a milder version of barbecue sauce, leave it out altogether.

STEP 1

STEP 2

STEP 3

STEP 4

# CITRUS & FRESH HERB MARINADES

*Choose one of these marinades to give a marvellous flavor to the food that is to be barbecued. Or just use them for brushing on to the food while it cooks over the hot coals.*

EACH DRESSING SERVES 4

*ORANGE, CHIVE & MARJORAM:*
*1 orange*
*¹/₂ cup olive oil*
*4 tbsp dry white wine*
*4 tbsp white wine vinegar*
*1 tbsp snipped fresh chives*
*1 tbsp chopped fresh marjoram*
*salt and pepper*

*THAI-SPICED LIME & CILANTRO:*
*1 stalk lemon grass*
*finely grated rind and juice of 1 lemon*
*4 tbsp sesame oil*
*2 tbsp light soy sauce*
*pinch ground ginger*
*1 tbsp chopped fresh cilantro*
*salt and pepper*

*BASIL, LEMON & OREGANO:*
*finely grated rind of 1 lemon*
*4 tbsp lemon juice*
*1 tbsp balsamic vinegar*
*2 tbsp red wine vinegar*
*2 tbsp virgin olive oil*
*1 tbsp chopped fresh oregano*
*1 tbsp chopped fresh basil*
*salt and pepper*

**1** To make the Orange, Chive & Marjoram Marinade, remove the rind from the orange with a zester, or grate it finely, then squeeze the juice.

**2** Mix the orange rind and juice with all the remaining ingredients in a small bowl, whisking together to combine. Season with salt and pepper.

**3** To make the Thai-spiced Lime & Cilantro Marinade, bruise the lemon grass by crushing it with a rolling pin. Mix the remaining ingredients together and add the lemon grass.

**4** To make the Basil, Lemon & Oregano Marinade, whisk all the ingredients together in a small bowl. Season with salt and pepper.

**5** Keep the marinades covered with plastic wrap or store in screw-top jars, ready for using as marinades or bastes.

STEP 1

STEP 2

STEP 3

STEP 4

# THREE FAVORITE DRESSINGS

*You can rely on any one of these delicious dressings to bring out the very best in your salads.*

EACH DRESSING SERVES 4

*WHOLEGRAIN MUSTARD & CIDER
VINEGAR DRESSING:*
*1/2 cup olive oil*
*4 tbsp cider vinegar*
*2 tsp wholegrain mustard*
*1/2 tsp superfine sugar*
*salt and pepper*

*GARLIC & PARSLEY DRESSING:*
*1 small garlic clove*
*1 tbsp fresh parsley*
*2/3 cup light cream*
*4 tbsp natural yogurt*
*1 tsp lemon juice*
*pinch superfine sugar*
*salt and pepper*

*RASPBERRY & HAZELNUT
VINAIGRETTE:*
*4 tbsp raspberry vinegar*
*4 tbsp light olive oil*
*4 tbsp hazelnut oil*
*1/2 tsp superfine sugar*
*2 tsp chopped fresh chives*
*salt and pepper*

**1** To make the Wholegrain Mustard & Cider Vinegar Dressing, whisk all the ingredients together in a small bowl.

**2** To make the Garlic & Parsley Dressing, crush the garlic clove and finely chop the parsley.

**3** Mix the garlic and parsley with the remaining ingredients. Whisk together until combined, then cover and chill for 30 minutes.

**4** To make the Raspberry & Hazelnut Vinaigrette, whisk all the ingredients together until combined.

**5** Keep the dressings covered with plastic wrap or sealed in screw-top jars. Chill until ready for use.

### PERFECT COMBINATIONS

Wholegrain Mustard & Cider Vinegar Dressing is excellent with a tomato salad. Garlic & Parsley Dressing tastes delicious as a coating for potato salad and Raspberry & Hazelnut Vinaigrette makes a superb dressing for mixed salad greens.

# CHAPTER TWELVE

# *Filled Things*

Easy-to-eat food is essential for barbecues. More often than not, barbecued food is eaten while standing up and moving around, and it is tricky trying to balance a plate, eat from it, hold a glass and have a conversation at the same time! Hopefully, the ideas in this section will help to make the balancing-act a little easier.

By providing a range of filled foods such as pitta and naan breads, French sticks, potatoes, burger buns and the occasional stuffed vegetable, you will be offering self-contained food that is easy to eat and enjoy – a movable feast! What's more, these ideas are perfect for children, who never seem to sit still for a moment.

The choices offered in this section are deliciously different and very tasty. Try, for instance, the Naan Bread with Curried Vegetable Kebabs on page 178 – a mouthwatering recipe for barbecued kebabs brushed with a spicy combination of cilantro, cumin and chili powder blended in natural yogurt. Served with Indian bread warmed over the hot coals, it really is a winner.

Opposite: *The setting sun provides a perfect backdrop for an unforgettable barbecue.*

**STEP 1**

**STEP 2**

**STEP 3**

**STEP 4**

# FILLED POTATOES

*Cook these potatoes conventionally, then wrap them in foil and keep them warm at the edge of the barbecue, ready to fill with a choice of three inspired mixtures.*

EACH DRESSING SERVES **4**

*4 large or 8 medium baking potatoes*

MEXICAN CORN RELISH:
*8-oz can corn, drained*
*1/2 red bell pepper, cored, deseeded and
    finely chopped*
*2-inch piece English cucumber,
    finely chopped*
*1/2 tsp chili powder*
*salt and pepper*

BLUE CHEESE, CELERY &
    CHIVE FILLING:
*1/2 cup full-fat soft cheese*
*1/2 cup natural fromage frais*
*4 oz Danish blue cheese, cut into cubes*
*1 celery stalk, finley chopped*
*2 tsp snipped fresh chives*
*celery salt and pepper*

MUSHROOMS IN SPICY
    TOMATO SAUCE:
*2 tbsp butter or margarine*
*8 oz button mushrooms*
*2/3 cup natural yogurt*
*1 tbsp tomato paste*
*2 tsp mild curry powder*
*salt and pepper*
*paprika or chili powder, or chopped fresh
    herbs, to garnish*

**1** Scrub the potatoes and prick them with a fork. Bake in a preheated oven at 400°F for about 1 hour until just tender.

**2** To make the Mexican Corn Relish, put half the corn into a bowl. Put the remainder into a blender or food processor for 10–15 seconds or chop and mash roughly by hand. Add the processed corn paste to the corn kernels with the bell pepper, cucumber and chili powder. Season to taste.

**3** To make the Blue Cheese, Celery & Chive Filling, mix the soft cheese and fromage frais together until smooth. Add the blue cheese, celery and chives. Season with pepper and celery salt.

**4** To make the Mushrooms in Spicy Tomato Sauce, melt the butter or margarine in a small skillet. Add the mushrooms and cook gently for 3–4 minutes. Remove from the heat and stir in the yogurt, tomato paste and curry powder. Season to taste.

**5** Wrap the cooked potatoes in foil and keep warm at the edge of the barbecue. Serve the fillings sprinkled with paprika or chili powder or herbs.

**STEP 1**

**STEP 2**

**STEP 3**

**STEP 4**

# MELTING CHEESE & ONION FRENCH STICKS

*Part-baked French sticks are split and filled with a tasty cheese and onion mixture, then wrapped in foil and cooked over the barbecue to make them warm, crisp and delicious.*

SERVES 4

4 part-baked French sticks
2 tbsp tomato relish
¼ cup butter
8 scallions, trimmed and finely chopped
½ cup cream cheese
1 cup grated Cheddar cheese
1 tsp snipped fresh chives
pepper

TO SERVE:
mixed salad greens
fresh herbs

**1** Split the part-baked French sticks in half lengthwise, without cutting right through. Spread a little tomato relish on each split loaf.

**2** Melt the butter in a skillet and add the scallions. Fry them gently until softened and golden. Remove from the heat and let cool slightly.

**3** Beat the cream cheese in a mixing bowl to soften it. Mix in the scallions, with any remaining butter. Add the grated cheese and snipped chives, and mix well. Season.

**4** Divide the cheese mixture between the French sticks, spread it over the cut surfaces and sandwich together. Wrap each French stick tightly in foil.

**5** Heat the French sticks over the barbecue for about 10–15 minutes, turning them occasionally. Peel back the foil to check that they are cooked and the cheese mixture has melted. Serve with salad greens and garnished with fresh herbs.

### TIME SAVER

If there's no room on the barbecue, and you want to eat these at the same time as the rest of the food, bake them in a preheated oven at 400°F for 15 minutes.

# CHEESEBURGERS IN BUNS WITH BARBECUE SAUCE

*Soya mince and seasonings combine to make these tasty vegetarian burgers, which are topped with cheese, tasty barbecue sauce, dill cucumber and tomato.*

STEP 1

SERVES 4

²/₃ cup dehydrated soya mince
1¼ cups vegetable stock
1 small onion, finely chopped
1 cup all-purpose flour
1 egg, beaten
1 tbsp chopped fresh herbs
1 tbsp mushroom ketchup or soy sauce
2 tbsp vegetable oil
4 burger buns
4 cheese slices
salt and pepper
lettuce, English cucumber and scallion salad,
    to serve

TO GARNISH:
1 quantity Tasty Barbecue Sauce
    (see page 164)
dill pickle
tomato slices

**1** Put the soy mince into a large bowl. Pour over the vegetable stock and let soak for about 15 minutes until it has been absorbed.

**2** Add the onion, flour, beaten egg and chopped herbs. Season with the mushroom ketchup or soy sauce and a little salt and pepper.

**3** Form the mixture into 8 burgers. Cover and chill until ready to cook.

**4** Brush the burgers with vegetable oil and barbecue them over hot coals, turning once. Allow about 5 minutes on each side.

**5** Split the buns and top with a burger. Lay a cheese slice on top and garnish with barbecue sauce, dill pickle and tomato slices. Serve with a green salad made with lettuce, scallion and cucumber.

STEP 2

STEP 3

### VARIATIONS

Flavor the burgers with different fresh herbs to vary the taste, or use mixed dried herbs for convenience.

Give the burgers a spicy flavor by adding ½–1 teaspoon chili powder to the mixture.

STEP 5

STEP 1

STEP 2

STEP 3

STEP 4

# NAAN BREAD WITH CURRIED VEGETABLE KEBABS

*Warmed Indian bread is served with barbecued vegetable kebabs, which are brushed with a curry-spiced yogurt baste.*

**SERVES 4**

*4 metal or wooden skewers (soak wooden skewers in warm water for 30 minutes)*

*YOGURT BASTE:*
*²/₃ cup natural yogurt*
*1 tbsp chopped fresh mint or 1 tsp dried mint*
*1 tsp ground cumin*
*1 tsp ground coriander*
*¹/₂ tsp chili powder*
*pinch turmeric*
*pinch ground ginger*
*salt and pepper*

*KEBABS:*
*8 small new potatoes*
*1 small eggplant*
*1 zucchini, cut into chunks*
*8 crimini or closed-cup*
   *mushrooms*
*8 small tomatoes*
*naan bread, to serve*
*fresh mint sprigs, to garnish*

**1** To make the spiced yogurt baste, mix together the yogurt, mint, cumin, coriander, chili powder, turmeric and ginger. Season with salt and pepper. Cover and chill.

**2** Boil the potatoes until just tender. Meanwhile, chop the eggplant into chunks and sprinkle them liberally with salt. Leave for 10–15 minutes to extract the bitter juices. Rinse and drain them well. Drain the potatoes.

**3** Thread the vegetables on to the skewers, alternating the different types.

**4** Place them in a shallow dish and brush with the yogurt baste, coating them evenly. Cover and chill until ready to cook.

**5** Wrap the naan bread in foil and place towards one side of the barbecue to warm through.

**6** Cook the kebabs over the barbecue, basting with any remaining spiced yogurt until they just begin to char slightly. Serve with the warmed Indian bread, garnished with sprigs of fresh mint.

STEP 1

STEP 2

STEP 3

STEP 4

# MEDITERRANEAN STUFFED BELL PEPPERS

*Halved bell peppers are stuffed with the flavors of the Mediterranean in this sunshine-bright dish.*

SERVES 4

1 red bell pepper, cored and deseeded
1 green bell pepper, cored and deseeded
1 yellow bell pepper, cored and deseeded
1 orange bell pepper, cored and deseeded
6 tbsp olive oil
1 small red onion, sliced
1 small eggplant, roughly chopped
4 oz button mushrooms, wiped
1 cup cherry tomatoes, halved
few drops mushroom ketchup
handful fresh basil leaves, torn into pieces
2 tbsp lemon juice
salt and pepper
fresh basil sprigs, to garnish
lemon wedges, to serve

**1** Halve the bell peppers, and sprinkle over a few drops of olive oil and season with a little salt and pepper.

**2** Heat the remaining olive oil in a skillet. Add the onion, eggplant and mushrooms, and fry for 3–4 minutes, stirring frequently. Remove from the heat and transfer to a mixing bowl.

**3** Add the cherry tomatoes, mushroom ketchup, basil leaves and lemon juice to the eggplant mixture. Season well with salt and pepper.

**4** Spoon the eggplant mixture into the bell pepper halves. Enclose in foil packages and cook over the hot coals for about 15–20 minutes, turning once.

**5** Unwrap carefully and serve garnished with sprigs of fresh basil. Serve with lemon wedges.

### TIPS

These stuffed bell peppers can be made in advance and kept in the refrigerator, wrapped in foil, ready for cooking over the barbecue.

Dried herbs can be used instead of fresh ones if they are unavailable. Substitute 1 teaspoon of dried basil or use mixed dried Italian herbs as an alternative.

If you wish, top these stuffed bell peppers with grated Mozzarella or Cheddar cheese – 1/4 cup will be sufficient.

STEP 1

STEP 2

STEP 3

STEP 4

# PITTA BREADS WITH GREEK SALAD & HOT ROSEMARY DRESSING

*Pitta breads are warmed over the hot coals, then split and filled with a Greek salad tossed in a fragrant rosemary dressing.*

SERVES 4

*½ iceberg lettuce, roughly chopped*
*2 large tomatoes, cut into wedges*
*3-inch piece English cucumber, cut into chunks*
*¼ cup pitted black olives*
*125 g/4 oz Feta cheese*
*4 pitta breads*

DRESSING:
*6 tbsp olive oil*
*3 tbsp red wine vinegar*
*1 tbsp crushed fresh rosemary*
*½ tsp superfine sugar*
*salt and pepper*

**1** To make the salad, combine the lettuce, tomatoes, cucumber and olives.

**2** Cut the Feta cheese into chunks and add to the salad. Toss gently.

**3** To make the dressing, whisk together the olive oil, red wine vinegar, rosemary and sugar. Season to taste with salt and pepper. Place in a small saucepan or heatproof bowl and heat gently or place over the barbecue to warm through.

**4** Wrap the pitta breads tightly in foil and place over the hot barbecue for 2–3 minutes, turning once, to warm through.

**5** Unwrap the breads and split them open. Fill with the salad mixture and drizzle over the warm dressing. Serve at once.

## TIPS

Substitute different herbs for the rosemary – either oregano or basil would make a delicious alternative.

Pack plenty of the salad into the pitta breads – they taste much better when packed full to bursting!

# CHAPTER THIRTEEN

# Main Courses

If you thought that vegetarian barbecues consisted of chargrilled mushroom kebabs, then these recipes will convince you to think again. True, mushrooms do make an appearance in a tempting recipe for brochettes, where they are combined with smoked tofu and basted with olive oil, lemon juice and garlic to make them taste really special. But how about Grilled Cypriot Cheese with Tomato & Red Onion Salad, Barbecued Bean Pot, or Grape Leaf Packages with Soft Cheese & Almonds? Throughout this chapter you will find appealing and imaginative recipes that will really spice up your barbecue!

Some preparation is needed before the barbecue starts, so that certain foods are soaking up their marinades, or are threaded on to skewers in readiness for cooking. The Barbecued Bean Pot needs to be pre-cooked in a conventional oven; the pot is then kept hot over the coals, ready for serving cowboy-style to your hungry guests.

All these recipes provide their fair share of protein – either from cheese, beans, garbanzo beans or tofu. And because they all contain vegetables of some description, they supply important vitamins, minerals and carbohydrates to the diet. Which all adds up to a bonus for food that tastes good too!

*Opposite: Use as wide a range of fresh vegetables as you can to create exotic and unusual dishes for your guests.*

STEP 1

STEP 2

STEP 3

STEP 4

# MOZZARELLA WITH BARBECUED RADICCIO

*Sliced Mozzarella is served with sliced tomatoes and radiccio, which is singed over hot coals and drizzled with a basil, olive oil and pesto dressing.*

SERVES 4

*1 tbsp red or green pesto sauce*
*6 tbsp virgin olive oil*
*3 tbsp red wine vinegar*
*handful fresh basil leaves*
*1 lb Mozzarella cheese*
*4 large tomatoes, sliced*
*2 radiccio*
*salt and pepper*
*fresh basil leaves, to garnish*

**1** To make the dressing, mix the pesto sauce, olive oil and red wine vinegar together.

**2** Tear the fresh basil leaves into tiny pieces and add them to the dressing. Season with a little salt and pepper.

**3** Slice the Mozzarella thinly and arrange it on 4 serving plates with the tomatoes.

**4** Leaving the root end on the radiccio, slice each one into quarters. Barbecue them quickly, so that the leaves singe on the outside. Place 2 quarters on each serving plate.

**5** Drizzle the dressing over the radiccio, cheese and tomatoes.

**6** Garnish with extra basil leaves and serve immediately.

### TIPS

When singeing the radiccio, it is a good idea to barbecue each quarter individually, holding it over the hot coals with tongs and turning it constantly.

If you can't find fresh basil, substitute oregano or marjoram instead. Tearing the basil leaves instead of chopping them helps to retain their peppery fragrance and flavor.

Pesto sauce is an aromatic paste, made from olive oil, basil and pine nuts, that can be bought in jars from supermarkets or delicatessens.

STEP 2

STEP 3

STEP 4

STEP 5

# SMOKED TOFU & MUSHROOM BROCHETTES

*These tofu and mushroom kebabs are marinated in a lemon, garlic and herb mixture so they soak up a delicious flavor.*

SERVES 4

8 wooden skewers
1 lemon
1 garlic clove, crushed
4 tbsp olive oil
4 tbsp white wine vinegar
1 tbsp chopped fresh herbs, such as
   rosemary, parsley and thyme
10 oz smoked tofu
12 oz cup mushrooms, wiped
salt and pepper
fresh herbs, to garnish

TO SERVE:
mixed salad greens
cherry tomatoes, halved

**1** Soak the wooden skewers in hand-hot water for 30 minutes.

**2** Finely grate the rind from the lemon and squeeze out the juice.

**3** Add the garlic, olive oil, vinegar and herbs to the lemon rind and juice, mixing well. Season to taste.

**4** Slice the tofu into large chunks. Thread the pieces on to kebab sticks or wooden skewers, alternating them with the mushrooms.

**5** Lay the kebabs in a shallow dish and pour over the marinade. Cover and chill for 1–2 hours, turning the kebabs in the marinade from time to time.

**6** Cook the kebabs over the barbecue, brushing them with the marinade and turning often, for about 6 minutes.

**7** Garnish with fresh herbs and serve with mixed salad greens and cherry tomatoes.

### EXTRA FLAVOR

Firm tofu can be substituted for the smoked variety if you prefer.

   Thread small fresh bay leaves on to the skewers. They will help to give the kebabs a good flavor.

STEP 1

STEP 2

STEP 3

STEP 5

# GRAPE LEAF PACKAGES WITH SOFT CHEESE & ALMONDS

*A wonderful combination of soft cheese, chopped dates, ground almonds and lightly fried nuts is encased in grape leaves, which are then wrapped in foil and cooked over the barbecue.*

SERVES 4

1¼ cups full-fat soft cheese
¼ cup ground almonds
2 tbsp dates, pitted and chopped
2 tbsp butter
¼ cup slivered almonds
12–16 grape leaves
salt and pepper

TO GARNISH:
rosemary sprigs
tomato wedges

**1** Beat the soft cheese in a large bowl to soften it.

**2** Add the ground almonds and chopped dates, and mix together thoroughly. Season with salt and pepper.

**3** Melt the butter in a small skillet. Add the slivered almonds and fry them gently for 2–3 minutes until golden brown. Remove from the heat and let cool for a few minutes.

**4** Mix the fried nuts with the soft cheese mixture, stirring well to combine thoroughly.

**5** Soak the grape leaves in water to remove some of the saltiness, if specified on the package. Drain them, lay them out on a counter and spoon an equal amount of the soft cheese mixture on to each one. Fold over the leaves to enclose the filling.

**6** Wrap the grape leaf packages in foil, 1 or 2 per foil package. Place over the barbecue to heat through for about 8–10 minutes, turning once.

**7** Serve with barbecued baby corn and garnish with sprigs of rosemary and tomato wedges.

### VARIATION

Omit the dates from the filling and substitute golden raisins or raisins. Ground and whole hazelnuts can be used instead of almonds.

# TURKISH VEGETABLE KEBABS WITH SPICY GARBANZO BEAN SAUCE

*A spicy garbanzo bean sauce is served with barbecued vegetable kebabs.*

STEP 1

### SERVES 4

*4 metal or wooden skewers (soak wooden skewers in warm water for 30 minutes)*

*SAUCE:*
*4 tbsp olive oil*
*3 garlic cloves, crushed*
*1 small onion, finely chopped*
*15-oz can garbanzo beans, rinsed and drained*
*1¼ cups natural yogurt*
*1 tsp cumin*
*½ tsp chili powder*
*lemon juice*
*salt and pepper*

*KEBABS:*
*1 eggplant*
*1 red bell pepper, cored and deseeded*
*1 green bell pepper, cored and deseeded*
*4 plum tomatoes*
*1 lemon, cut into wedges*
*8 small fresh bay leaves*
*olive oil for brushing*

**1** To make the sauce, heat the olive oil in a small skillet and fry the garlic and onion gently for about 5 minutes until softened and golden brown.

**2** Put the garbanzo beans and yogurt into a blender or food processor and add the cumin, chili powder and onion mixture. Blend for about 15 seconds until smooth. Alternatively, mash the garbanzo beans and mix with the yogurt, cumin, chili powder and onion.

STEP 2

**3** Tip the processed or mashed mixture into a bowl and season to taste with lemon juice, salt and pepper. Cover and chill until ready to serve.

**4** To prepare the kebabs, cut the vegetables into large chunks and thread them on to the skewers, placing a bay leaf and lemon wedge at both ends of each kebab.

STEP 3

**5** Brush the kebabs with olive oil and cook them over the barbecue, turning frequently, for 5–8 minutes. Heat the garbanzo bean sauce and serve with the kebabs.

### MILDER SAUCE

To make a sauce with a milder flavor, substitute paprika for the chili powder.

STEP 4

STEP 1

STEP 2

STEP 3

STEP 4

# BARBECUED BEAN POT

*Cook this tasty vegetable and soy protein casserole conventionally, then keep it piping hot over the barbecue. Its delicious aroma will cut through the fresh air to make appetites very keen!*

SERVES 4

*¼ cup butter or margarine*
*1 large onion, chopped*
*2 garlic cloves, crushed*
*2 carrots, sliced*
*2 celery stalks, sliced*
*1 tbsp paprika*
*2 tsp ground cumin*
*14-oz can chopped tomatoes*
*15-oz can mixed beans, rinsed*
*    and drained*
*⅔ cup vegetable stock*
*1 tbsp molasses sugar or molasses*
*12 oz soy cubes*
*salt and pepper*

**1** Melt the butter or margarine in a large flameproof casserole and fry the onion and garlic gently for about 5 minutes, until golden brown.

**2** Add the carrots and celery and cook for a further 2 minutes, then stir in the paprika and cumin.

**3** Add the tomatoes and beans. Pour in the stock and add the sugar or(molasses. Bring to the boil, then reduce the heat and simmer, uncovered, for 30 minutes, stirring occasionally.

**4** Add the soy cubes to the casserole and cook, covered, for a further 20 minutes. Stir the mixture occasionally.

**5** Season to taste, then transfer the casserole to the barbecue, keeping it to one side to keep hot.

**6** Ladle on to plates and serve with crusty French bread.

### ALTERNATIVES

If you prefer, cook the casserole in a preheated oven at 375°F from step 3, but keep the dish covered.

Instead of mixed beans you could use just one type of canned beans. Choose from red kidney beans, black-eyed peas, garbanzo beans or soy beans.

STEP 2

STEP 3

STEP 4

STEP 6

# GRILLED CYPRIOT CHEESE WITH TOMATO & RED ONION SALAD

*Haloumi is a type of Cypriot cheese which remains firm and takes on a marvellous flavor when swiftly barbecued.*

SERVES 4

1 lb Haloumi cheese
¹/₂ quantity Orange, Chive & Marjoram
  Marinade (see page 166)

SALAD:
8 oz plum tomatoes
1 small red onion
4 tbsp olive oil
2 tbsp cider vinegar
1 tsp lemon juice
pinch ground coriander
2 tsp chopped fresh cilantro
salt and pepper
fresh basil leaves, to garnish

**1** Slice the cheese quite thickly and place it in a shallow dish.

**2** Pour the marinade over the cheese. Cover and chill for at least 30 minutes.

**3** To make the salad, slice the tomatoes and arrange them on a serving plate. Thinly slice the onion and scatter over the tomatoes.

**4** Whisk together the olive oil, vinegar, lemon juice, ground coriander and fresh cilantro. Season to

**5** taste with salt and pepper, then drizzle the dressing over the tomatoes and onions. Cover and chill.

**6** Drain the marinade from the Haloumi cheese. Cook the cheese over hot coals for 2 minutes, turning once. Lift on to plates and serve with the salad.

### SERVING SUGGESTIONS

Warmed pitta breads taste wonderful stuffed with the salad and topped with the barbecued Haloumi.

If Haloumi cheese is not available, you can use Feta cheese instead.

Serve the cheese and salad with crusty bread or potato salad to make it more filling.

# CHAPTER FOURTEEN

# *Salads*

Lively salads are an essential accompaniment to barbecued food, supplying a pleasant change of taste and texture to refresh the palate. For something easy and quick to make, you could simply prepare a huge bowl of mixed salad greens, drizzled with one of the dressings from page 168, but here you will discover some new ideas for more unusual combinations.

These days it is so easy to make exciting salads with interesting ingredients. All year round, supermarkets and shops are full of glorious vegetables and fruits from all over the world. We can make the most of seasonal, home-grown produce for flavor and economy, or we can buy imported foods for special occasions, or to perk up everyday ingredients to transform them into something special. We can certainly enjoy eating salads throughout the year, even if we can't always rely on the weather for a barbecue!

Any salad is only as good as the ingredients that you put into it, so be sure to choose produce from a reputable supplier, and use it when it is at its best. That way you will be making the most of its freshness and flavor, and you will be getting all the goodness that the fruit and vegetables contain.

Opposite: *Fresh fruits and vegetables used in a range of imaginative salads will provide a refreshing accompaniment to the main course dishes.*

STEP 1

STEP 2

STEP 3

STEP 4

# CHARGRILLED VEGETABLES WITH SIDEKICK DRESSING

*Colorful vegetables are barbecued over hot coals to make this unusual hot salad, which is served with a spicy chili sauce on the side.*

SERVES 4

1 red bell pepper, cored and deseeded
1 orange or yellow bell pepper, cored
   and deseeded
2 zucchini
2 corn-on-the-cob
1 eggplant
olive oil for brushing
chopped fresh thyme, rosemary and parsley
salt and pepper
lime or lemon wedges, to serve

DRESSING:
2 tbsp olive oil
1 tbsp sesame oil
1 garlic clove, crushed
1 small onion, finely chopped
1 celery stalk, finely chopped
1 small green chili, deseeded and
   finely chopped
4 tomatoes, chopped
2-inch piece English cucumber,
   finely chopped
1 tbsp tomato paste
1 tbsp lime or lemon juice

**1** To make the dressing, heat the olive and sesame oils together in a saucepan or skillet. Add the garlic and onion and fry together gently for about 3 minutes until softened.

**2** Add the celery, chili and tomatoes to the pan and cook, stirring occasionally, for 5 minutes over a medium heat.

**3** Stir in the cucumber, tomato paste and lime or lemon juice, and simmer for 8–10 minutes until thick and pulpy. Season to taste with salt and pepper.

**4** Cut the vegetables into thick slices and brush with a little olive oil.

**5** Cook the vegetables over the hot coals for 5-8 minutes, sprinkling them with salt and pepper and fresh herbs as they cook, and turning once.

**6** Divide the vegetables between 4 serving plates and spoon some of the dressing on to the side. Serve at once, sprinkled with a few more chopped herbs and accompanied by the lime or lemon wedges.

STEP 1

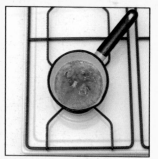

STEP 2

STEP 3

STEP 4

# GOAT'S CHEESE WITH WALNUTS IN WARM OIL & VINEGAR DRESSING

*This delicious salad combines soft goat's cheese with walnut halves. Served on a bed of mixed salad greens and sprinkled with a warm walnut oil and wine vinegar dressing, it can double as an appetizer.*

SERVES 4

1 cup walnut halves
mixed salad greens
4 oz soft goat's cheese
snipped fresh chives, to garnish

*DRESSING:*
6 tbsp walnut oil
3 tbsp white wine vinegar
1 tbsp clear honey
1 tsp Dijon mustard
pinch of ground ginger
salt and pepper

**1** To make the dressing, whisk together the walnut oil, wine vinegar, honey, mustard and ginger in a small saucepan. Season to taste.

**2** Heat the dressing on the stove top or over the barbecue, stirring occasionally, until warm. Add the walnut halves to the warm dressing and continue to heat for 3–4 minutes.

**3** Arrange the salad leaves on 4 serving plates and place spoonfuls of goat's cheese on top. Lift the walnut halves from the dressing with a perforated spoon, and scatter them over the salads.

**4** Transfer the warm dressing to a small jug, for sprinkling over the salads.

**5** Sprinkle chives over the salads and serve them, accompanied by the warm walnut oil dressing.

TIPS

Hazelnut oil makes a delicious alternative to walnut oil; if you use it, you can also replace the walnuts with hazelnuts if you wish.

If you are heating the dressing over the barbecue, choose an old saucepan, as it may become blackened on the outside.

# CARROT & CASHEW NUT COLESLAW

*This simple salad has a brilliant dressing made from poppy seeds pan-fried in sesame oil to bring out their flavor.*

STEP 1

SERVES 4

1 large carrot, grated
1 small onion, finely chopped
2 celery stalks, chopped
1/4 small, hard white cabbage, shredded
1 tbsp chopped fresh parsley
4 tbsp sesame oil
1/2 tsp poppy seeds
1/2 cup cashew nuts
2 tbsp white wine or cider vinegar
salt and pepper
fresh parsley sprigs, to garnish

**1** In a large salad bowl, mix together the carrot, onion, celery and cabbage. Stir in the chopped parsley.

**2** Heat the sesame oil in a saucepan that has a lid. Add the poppy seeds and cover the pan. Cook over a medium high heat until the seeds start to make a popping sound. Remove from the heat and let cool.

**3** Scatter the cashew nuts onto a cookie sheet. Place them under a medium-hot broiler and toast until lightly browned, being careful not to burn them. Let cool.

**4** Add the vinegar to the oil and poppy seeds, then pour over the carrot mixture. Add the cooled cashew nuts. Toss together to coat the salad ingredients with the dressing.

**5** Garnish the salad with sprigs of parsley and serve.

STEP 2

STEP 3

### VARIATIONS

Sesame seeds or sunflower seeds can be used in place of poppy seeds.

Substitute peanuts for cashew nuts if you prefer – they are more economical and taste every bit as good when lightly toasted.

STEP 4

STEP 1

STEP 2

STEP 3

STEP 4

# HONEYDEW & STRAWBERRY SALAD WITH COOL CUCUMBER DRESSING

*This refreshing fruit-based salad is perfect for a hot summer's day.*

SERVES 4

*¹/₂ iceberg lettuce, shredded*
*1 small honeydew melon*
*1¹/₂ cups strawberries, hulled and sliced*
*2-inch piece English cucumber, thinly sliced*
*fresh mint sprigs, to garnish*

*DRESSING:*
*scant 1 cup natural yogurt*
*2-inch piece English cucumber, peeled*
*a few fresh mint leaves*
*¹/₂ tsp finely grated lime or lemon rind*
*pinch superfine sugar*
*3–4 ice cubes*

**1** Arrange the shredded lettuce on 4 serving plates.

**2** Cut the melon lengthwise into quarters. Scoop out the seeds and cut through the flesh down to the skin at 1-inch intervals. Cut the melon close to the skin and detach the flesh.

**3** Place the chunks of melon on the bed of lettuce with the strawberries and cucumber.

**4** To make the dressing, put the yogurt, cucumber, mint leaves, lime or lemon rind, superfine sugar and

ice cubes into a blender or food processor. Blend together for about 15 seconds until smooth. Alternatively, chop the cucumber and mint finely, crush the ice cubes and combine with the other ingredients.

**5** Serve the salad with a little dressing poured over it. Garnish with sprigs of fresh mint.

### VARIATIONS

Omit the ice cubes in the dressing if you prefer, but make sure that the ingredients are well chilled. This will ensure that the finished dressing is really cool.

Charentais, cantaloup or ogen melon can be substituted for honeydew.

STEP 1

STEP 2

STEP 3

STEP 4

# THREE-WAY POTATO SALAD

*There's nothing to beat the flavour of new potatoes, served just warm in a delicious dressing.*

EACH DRESSING SERVES 4

*1lb new potatoes for each dressing*
*fresh herbs, to garnish*

LIGHT CURRY DRESSING:
*1 tbsp vegetable oil*
*1 tbsp medium curry paste*
*1 small onion, chopped*
*1 tbsp mango chutney, chopped*
*6 tbsp natural yogurt*
*3 tbsp light cream*
*2 tbsp mayonnaise*
*salt and pepper*
*1 tbsp light cream, to garnish*

WARM VINAIGRETTE DRESSING:
*6 tbsp hazelnut oil*
*3 tbsp cider vinegar*
*1 tsp wholegrain mustard*
*1 tsp superfine sugar*
*few basil leaves, torn into shreds*
*salt and pepper*

PARSLEY, SCALLION & SOURED
   CREAM DRESSING:
*$^2/_3$ cup soured cream*
*3 tbsp light mayonnaise*
*4 scallions, trimmed and finely chopped*
*1 tbsp chopped fresh parsley*
*salt and pepper*

**1** To make the Light Curry Dressing, heat the vegetable oil in a saucepan and add the curry paste and onion. Fry together, stirring frequently, until the onion is soft, about 5 minutes. Remove from the heat and let cool slightly.

**2** Mix together the mango chutney, yogurt, cream and mayonnaise. Add the curry mixture and blend together. Season with salt and pepper.

**3** To make the Vinaigrette Dressing, whisk the hazelnut oil, cider vinegar, mustard, sugar and basil together in a small jug or bowl. Season.

**4** To make the Parsley, Scallion & Soured Cream Dressing, mix all the ingredients together until thoroughly combined. Season with salt and pepper.

**5** Cook the potatoes in lightly salted boiling water until just tender. Drain well and let cool for 5 minutes, then add the chosen dressing, tossing to coat. Serve, garnished with fresh herbs, spooning a little light cream on to the potatoes if you have used the curry dressing.

STEP 2

STEP 3

STEP 4

STEP 5

# DEEP SOUTH SPICED RICE & BEANS

*Cajun spices add a flavor of the American deep south to this colorful rice and red kidney bean salad.*

SERVES 4

scant 1 cup long-grain rice
4 tbsp olive oil
1 small green bell pepper, cored, deseeded
    and chopped
1 small red bell pepper, cored, deseeded
    and chopped
1 onion, finely chopped
1 small red or green chili, deseeded and
    finely chopped
2 tomatoes, chopped
$1/2$ cup canned red kidney beans, rinsed
    and drained
1 tbsp chopped fresh basil
2 tsp chopped fresh thyme, or 1 tsp dried
1 tsp Cajun spice
salt and pepper
fresh basil leaves, to garnish

**1** Cook the rice in plenty of boiling, lightly salted water for about 12 minutes until just tender. Rinse with cold water and drain well.

**2** Meanwhile, heat the olive oil in a skillet and fry the green and red bell peppers and onion together gently until softened, about 5 minutes.

**3** Add the chili and tomatoes, and cook for a further 2 minutes.

**4** Add the vegetable mixture and red kidney beans to the rice. Stir well to combine thoroughly.

**5** Stir the chopped herbs and Cajun spice into the rice mixture. Season well with salt and pepper, and serve, garnished with basil leaves.

## CHILIES

The fresh red or green chili can be replaced by 1 tsp chili powder, for speed and convenience.

    Take care when handling fresh chilies, as the residue from them can burn or irritate the skin. Be especially careful to avoid rubbing your eyes when preparing them, and rinse your hands well after handling them.

# CHAPTER FIFTEEN

# *Desserts*

By the time everyone at the barbecue has eaten their fill of main course foods, there is hardly any room left for dessert. But for those who are confirmed dessert-lovers, a meal would not seem complete without something to finish off with. The recipes in this chapter offer the ideal solution.

The dishes that follow in the next few pages are light, yet full of flavor. There are three recipes to cook over the coals, a couple of fresh fruit salad combinations and an easy recipe for Giggle Cake that will keep the children happy. They will also love the Banana & Marshmallow Melts that are served oozing with butterscotch sauce, and there is even a recipe for addicted chocoholics – a fabulous Hot Chocolate Dip that is served with tropical fruit kebabs. Remember to keep a jug of cream at the ready, and some ice cream in the freezer, just for those who can't resist an extra helping of indulgence.

Make two or three of the recipes here if you are planning to make a real day of your barbecue. And don't forget, people often wander back for seconds even if they thought they were full half an hour before. So make plenty, as all of these desserts are worth making room for!

Opposite: *Fresh fruits from home and abroad provide a delicious basis for some barbecued desserts.*

STEP 2

STEP 3

STEP 4

STEP 5

# BANANA & MARSHMALLOW MELTS WITH BUTTERSCOTCH SAUCE

*This simply delicious dessert will go down a treat with children of all ages. Bananas and marshmallows taste fantastic with the warm butterscotch sauce.*

SERVES 4

4 wooden skewers
4 bananas
4 tbsp lemon juice
8 oz marshmallows

SAUCE:
1/2 cup butter
2/3 cup light muscovado sugar
1/3 cup light corn syrup
4 tbsp hot water

**1** Soak the wooden skewers in tepid water for 30 minutes.

**2** Slice the bananas into large chunks and dip them into the lemon juice to prevent them from going brown.

**3** Thread the marshmallows and pieces of banana alternately on to kebab sticks or bamboo skewers, placing 2 marshmallows and 1 piece of banana on to each one.

**4** To make the sauce, melt the butter, sugar and syrup together in a small saucepan. Add the hot water, stirring until blended and smooth. Do not boil or else the mixture will become like toffee.

Keep the sauce warm at the edge of the barbecue, stirring from time to time.

**5** Sear the kebabs over the barbecue coals for 30–40 seconds, turning constantly, so that the marshmallows just begin to brown and melt.

**6** Serve the kebabs with some of the butterscotch sauce spooned over.

### SERVING SUGGESTIONS

The warm butterscotch sauce tastes wonderful with vanilla ice cream. Make double the quantity of sauce if you plan to serve ice cream at the barbecue.

Ideally, prepare the kebabs just before they are cooked to prevent the bananas from turning brown. The sauce can be prepared in advance, though.

You can heat whole bananas in their skins over the barbecue. When blackened, split the skins open and serve the bananas in their skins with a spoonful of the sauce.

STEP 1

STEP 2

STEP 3

STEP 4

# CHAR-COOKED PINEAPPLE WITH GINGER & BROWN SUGAR BUTTER

*Fresh pineapple slices are cooked on the barbecue, and brushed with a buttery fresh ginger and brown sugar baste.*

SERVES 4

1 fresh pineapple

BUTTER:
1/2 cup butter
1/2 cup light muscovado sugar
1 tsp finely grated fresh gingerroot

TOPPING:
1 cup natural fromage frais
1/2 tsp ground cinnamon
1 tbsp light muscovado sugar

**1** Prepare the fresh pineapple by cutting off the spiky top. Peel the pineapple with a sharp knife and cut into thick slices.

**2** To make the ginger-flavored butter, put the butter, sugar and ginger into a small saucepan and heat gently until melted. Transfer to a heatproof bowl and keep warm at the side of the barbecue, ready for basting the fruit.

**3** To prepare the topping, mix together the fromage frais, cinnamon and sugar. Cover and chill until ready to serve.

**4** Barbecue the pineapple slices for about 2 minutes on each side, brushing them with the ginger butter baste.

**5** Serve the pineapple with a little extra ginger butter sauce poured over. Top with a spoonful of the spiced fromage frais.

## VARIATIONS

If you prefer, substitute 1/2 teaspoon ground ginger for the grated fresh gingerroot.

Light muscovado sugar gives the best flavor, but you can use ordinary soft brown sugar instead.

You can make this dessert indoors by cooking the pineapple under a hot broiler, basting it as above with the melted ginger butter.

STEP 2

STEP 3

STEP 3

STEP 4

# TOASTED TROPICAL FRUIT KEBABS WITH HOT CHOCOLATE DIP

*Spear some chunks of exotic tropical fruits on to kebab sticks, sear them over the barbecue and serve with this amazing chocolate dip.*

SERVES 4

4 wooden skewers

DIP:
4 squares dark chocolate, broken
   into pieces
2 tbsp light corn syrup
1 tbsp cocoa powder
1 tbsp cornstarch
generous ¾ cup milk

KEBABS:
1 mango
1 papaya
2 kiwi fruit
½ small pineapple
1 large banana
2 tbsp lemon juice
⅔ cup white rum

**1** Soak the wooden skewers in tepid water for 30 minutes.

**2** Put all the ingredients for the chocolate dip into a saucepan. Heat, stirring constantly, until thickened and smooth. Keep warm at the edge of the barbecue.

**3** Slice the mango on each side of its large, flat pit. Cut the flesh into chunks, removing the peel. Halve, deseed and peel the papaya and cut it into chunks. Peel the kiwi fruit and slice into chunks. Peel and cut the pineapple into chunks. Peel and slice the banana and dip the pieces in the lemon juice.

**4** Thread the pieces of fruit alternately on to the wooden skewers. Place them in a shallow dish and pour over the rum. Let them soak up the flavor of the rum until ready to barbecue, at least 30 minutes.

**5** Cook the kebabs over the hot coals, turning frequently, until seared, about 2 minutes. Serve, accompanied by the hot chocolate dip.

### VARIATIONS

Milk chocolate can be used in the chocolate dip instead of dark, and honey could be substituted for light corn syrup.

For the kebabs, use any fruit you like, providing it can be threaded on to skewers. Peaches, nectarines, apples and grapes are all suitable.

# GIGGLE CAKE

*It's a mystery how this cake got its name – perhaps it's because it's easy to make and fun to eat. It takes only minutes to put together.*

STEP 1

STEP 2

SERVES 8

2 cups mixed dried fruit
¹/₂ cup butter or margarine
1 cup soft brown sugar
2 cups self-raising flour
pinch salt
2 eggs, beaten
7¹/₂-oz can chopped pineapple, drained
¹/₂ cup candied cherries, halved

**1** Put the mixed dried fruit into a large bowl and cover with boiling water. Let soak for 10–15 minutes, then drain well.

**2** Put the butter or margarine and sugar into a large saucepan and heat gently until melted. Add the drained mixed dried fruit and cook over a low heat, stirring frequently, for 4–5 minutes. Remove from the heat and transfer to a mixing bowl. Let cool.

**3** Sift the flour and salt into the fruit mixture and stir well. Add the eggs, mixing until thoroughly incorporated.

**4** Add the pineapples and cherries to the cake mixture and stir to combine. Transfer to a greased and lined 2 lb loaf pan and level the surface.

**5** Bake in a preheated oven at 350°F for about 1 hour. Test the cake with a fine skewer; if it comes out clean, the cake is cooked. If not, return to the oven for a few more minutes.

STEP 3

### VARIATIONS

If you wish, add 1 teaspoon apple pie spice to the cake mixture, sifting it in with the flour.

Bake the cake in an 7-inch round cake pan if you don't have a loaf pan of the right size. Remember to grease and line it first.

STEP 4

221

**STEP 1**

**STEP 2**

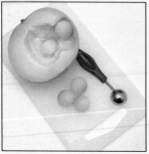

**STEP 3**

**STEP 5**

# GREEN FRUIT SALAD WITH MINT & LEMON SYRUP

*This delightful fresh fruit salad is the perfect finale for a summer barbecue. It has a lovely light syrup made with fresh mint and honey.*

**SERVES 4**

1 small Charentais or honeydew melon
2 green apples
2 kiwi fruit
1 cup seedless green grapes
fresh mint sprigs, to decorate

*SYRUP:*
*1 lemon*
*²/₃ cup white wine*
*²/₃ cup water*
*4 tbsp clear honey*
*fresh mint sprigs*

**1** To make the syrup, pare the rind from the lemon using a potato peeler.

**2** Put the lemon rind into a saucepan with the wine, water and honey. Heat and simmer gently for 10 minutes. Remove from the heat. Add the sprigs of mint and let cool.

**3** Slice the melon in half and scoop out the seeds. Use a melon baller or a teaspoon to make melon balls.

**4** Core and chop the apples. Peel and slice the kiwi fruit.

**5** Strain the cooled syrup into a serving bowl, removing and reserving the lemon rind and discarding the mint sprigs. Add the apple, grapes, kiwi and melon. Stir through gently to mix.

**6** Serve, decorated with sprigs of fresh mint and some of the reserved lemon rind.

## SERVING SUGGESTION

Serve the fruit salad in an attractive glass dish. Chill the dish for 20 minutes first, then keep the fruit salad cold by placing the dish in a large bowl of crushed ice or ice cubes.

STEP 1

STEP 2

STEP 3

STEP 4

# BLACKBERRY, APPLE & FRESH FIG COMPOTE WITH HONEY YOGURT

*Elderflower cordial is used in the syrup for this refreshing fruit compôte, giving it a delightfully summery flavor.*

SERVES 4

1 lemon
$^{1}/_{4}$ cup superfine sugar
4 tbsp elderflower cordial
1$^{1}/_{4}$ cups water
4 eating apples
2 cups blackberries
2 fresh figs

TOPPING:
$^{2}/_{3}$ cup thick natural yogurt
2 tbsp clear honey

**1** Pare the rind from the lemon using a potato peeler. Squeeze the juice. Put the lemon rind and juice into a saucepan with the sugar, elderflower cordial and water. Heat gently and simmer, uncovered, for 10 minutes.

**2** Peel, core and slice the apples, and add them to the saucepan. Simmer gently for about 4–5 minutes until just tender. Let cool.

**3** Transfer the apples and syrup to a serving bowl and add the blackberries. Slice and add the figs. Stir gently to mix. Cover and chill until ready to serve.

**4** Spoon the yogurt into a small serving bowl and drizzle the honey over the top. Cover and chill, then serve with the fruit salad.

### ELDERFLOWERS AND CREAM

Elderflower cordial is easy to obtain from supermarkets, health-food shops and delicatessens. Alternatively, you can use a blackberry or apple cordial instead. Do not prepare the apples until the syrup is ready, or they will begin to turn brown.

Fresh whipped cream is delicious served with this fruit salad. If you are choosing cream for whipping, buy either heavy cream or whipping cream. Double cream labelled as "extra thick" is only suitable for spooning, and will not whip.

# Vegetarian Cuisine

Vegetarian Nutrition 228

The Vegetarian Shopping Basket 229

The Vegetarian Store-cupboard 229

The Vegetarian Fridge and Freezer 231

Salads 231

Dressings 232

Salad Greens 233

Nuts 234

Vegetarian Food for Barbecues 235

Planning Your Barbecue 235

Safety Tips 236

Wok Cookery 236

Preparing Food for the Wok 236

Cooking Techniques 236

# VEGETARIAN CUISINE

## NUTRITION
Vegetarians eating a wide variety of foods should have no problem in obtaining enough B vitamins from their food, although vegans (who do not eat dairy products) need to include some sort of B12 supplement in their diet.

As vitamin C can be lost during cooking, you must take care when boiling vegetables to prevent its loss. Use a small amount of water to prevent the vitamin from leaching out.

Eat foods rich in vitamin C with iron-rich foods, as it helps to increase the uptake of iron; and avoid drinking tea, coffee and certain soft drinks with foods that contain vitamin C, as the caffeine can decrease how much vitamin C your body subsequently absorbs.

Vitamin D is often known as the "sunshine vitamin", as the body can manufacture its own supply from exposure to sunlight.

### Ingredients
To give variety and interest to your cooking, experiment with different seasonings, spices and herbs, and try out some of the wonderful array of oils and vinegars.

When choosing your rice, remember that brown rice is a better source of vitamin B1 and fiber.

## VEGETARIAN NUTRITION
People choose to eat vegetarian food for all sorts of different reasons, whether on moral grounds, for health reasons, for economy or simply because they prefer the flavor. These days, far more people choose to eat vegetarian food at least some of the time, to make an interesting change or to reduce their food bill.

Whatever the motive, one thing is certain – everyone enjoys good food, and vegetarian food can be as good as, and indeed often better than, the traditional meat and fish dishes. So dispel the myth that vegetarian cooking can be complicated, time-consuming, boring or heavy. Choose recipes which are fun to cook and eat, being full of vibrant colors and exciting flavors. Experiment with exotic fruit, vegetables, herbs and spices as well as the vast range of grains and pulses that are available. Vegetarian meals are perfect for entertaining or just for the family to enjoy, and can be easily adapted to suit all tastes.

### Getting the balance right
Vegetarian food is extremely healthy, and provides all the important vitamins, minerals, proteins, carbohydrates and fats that make up a nutritious, well-balanced diet. And because vegetarians tend to eat more fruit, vegetables, grains and pulses, the diet is rich in complex carbohydrates, the primary source of energy, and fiber, which helps to keep your body vibrant and healthy from the inside.

There is no problem in obtaining sufficient protein in a vegetarian diet – there are plenty of foods to choose from. Eggs, cheese, milk, nuts and beans, soy products such as TVP (texturized vegetable protein), soy milk and tofu, or mycoprotein are all excellent sources. Make sure that you eat a wide variety of these foods to get the full range of protein that your body needs.

One additional benefit of following a vegetarian diet is that it can be quite low in fat. The main sources of fat in your diet will be from vegetable, nut and olive oils, butter and margarine, nuts and any products containing these ingredients. So slimmers can succeed in losing weight following a vegetarian diet, provided they keep an eye on their overall fat intake. Complex carbohydrates such as brown rice, oats and whole wheat pasta are particularly useful to dieters, as they ensure a steady release of energy and a stable blood sugar level.

For supplies of vitamins in a vegetarian diet, you can't go far wrong. Fruit and vegetables are packed with important vitamins, essential for our general well-being and the healthy functioning of our bodies.

The best sources of vitamin A are yellow fruits and vegetables and some green vegetables – apricots, peaches, spinach and carrots, for example. It is also present in butter and added to margarines. Vitamin A helps us to resist infections and keeps skin, hair, eyes and body tissues healthy.

The B group vitamins aid the release of energy taken in as food, acting as a catalyst. They are also vital for the healthy maintenance of both the nervous system and red blood cells. Apart from vitamin B12, all the B vitamins can be found in yeast and wholegrain cereals, especially wheat flour and wheatgerm.

Vitamin C is well known for helping to prevent infections and is firmly believed by many to assist in warding off, as well as curing, winter colds and 'flu. It also plays an important role in assisting the absorption of iron. Fresh fruit, leafy vegetables, tomatoes, bell peppers and potatoes are all good sources.

The other important vitamin for good health is vitamin D. It enables the body to absorb calcium, thus providing strong bones and teeth. Good food sources include eggs, cheese, margarine and butter.

Minerals are the other vital nutrient. These elements are needed by the body in tiny amounts, but they are needed regularly, so it is wise to know about them and ensure that you include enough foods containing them in your diet. Calcium is found in milk, cheese, yogurt and other dairy products, leafy green vegetables, bread, nuts, seeds and dried fruits. Iron is found in beans, seeds, nuts, eggs, cocoa and chocolate, whole wheat bread, leafy green vegetables and dried fruits (especially apricots and figs). Other minerals important in the diet include magnesium, phosphorus, potassium and zinc, but there should be no problem in obtaining sufficient quantities of these elements as long as you eat a wide variety of foods.

## THE VEGETARIAN SHOPPING BASKET

When shopping for vegetarian foods, be sure that you are not buying animal products unawares. Choose cheese that is made from vegetarian rennet; buy agar-agar or gelozone instead of gelatine; select a vegetarian suet instead of beef suet – no, you won't have to forego delicious dumplings!

Be aware of what you are spreading on your bread too. Some margarines are not suitable as they contain both fish oils and animal fats, so check that you are buying one made entirely of vegetable oil. Butter is perfect, unless you are a vegan.

## THE VEGETARIAN STORE-CUPBOARD

A well-stocked store-cupboard forms the backbone of any good cook's kitchen, and it is always useful to have plenty of basic foods ready to hand. Use the following information as a checklist for when you need to replenish your dwindling stocks.

### Flours, grains, pasta and pulses

You will need to keep a selection of flours – all-purpose and self-raising flour if you want to make your own bread, and also whole wheat flour, for using on its own or for combining with white flour for cakes and pastries.

You may also like to keep some rice flour and cornstarch (from maize) for thickening sauces and to add to cakes, biscuits and puddings. Buckwheat, garbanzo bean and soy flours can also be bought – useful for pancakes and for combining with other flours to add different flavors and textures.

It is important to cook dried red and black kidney beans in plenty of vigorously boiling water for 15 minutes to destroy harmful toxins in the outer skin. Drain and rinse the beans, and then continue to simmer until the beans are tender. Soy beans should be boiled for 1 hour, as they contain a substance that inhibits protein absorption.

If you are short of time, canned beans will do just as well. Once opened, they will keep in the fridge for several days, but don't leave them in the tin – transfer them to a bowl, and cover them up.

Try grinding your own spices with a mortar and pestle, or in a coffee mill, to make your own blends, or just experiment with those that you can buy. Although spices will keep well, don't leave them in the cupboard for too long, as they may lose some of their strength.

To bring out the flavor of nuts and seeds, broil or roast them until lightly browned.

When buying dried fruits, look for those that have not been treated with anything: buy figs that have not been rolled in sugar, for example, and choose unsulphured apricots, if they are available.

### Oils and fats

Olive oil tastes wonderful as a basis for salad dressings. A fine fruity virgin oil from the first pressing makes a deliciously robust dressing, or choose a lighter oil to give a dressing with a more delicate flavor. It is a good tip to dress hot pasta with a couple of tablespoons of good quality home-made salad dressing. The flavor is absorbed, and it helps to prevent the pasta from sticking.

A good way of making the most of day-old French or Italian bread is to slice it, place it on a baking tray and drizzle it with olive oil. Top with sliced tomatoes, grated cheese and slivers of black olives, and then bake in a hot oven for a few minutes. When you are using oil in dressings or adding it to a wok or skillet, it is a good idea to measure it – one tablespoon of oil contains 120 calories. (One tablespoonful of butter or margarine contains 105 calories.) It is easy to use twice as much without realizing.

If you are trying to lose weight, reduce your fat intake where possible, not only by cutting down on the "visible" fats like oils, margarine and butter, but by trying to reduce the foods containing hidden fats, such as hard cheese, nuts, pastries, cakes and cookies. Watch those calorie-laden salad dressings and

Keep a good variety of grains – for rice choose from long-grain, basmati, Italian arborio for making risotto, short-grain for puddings, wild rice to add interest. Look out for fragrant Thai rice, jasmine rice and combinations of different varieties to add color and texture to your dishes.

Other grains add variety to the diet – try to include some barley (whole grain or pearl), millet, bulgur wheat, polenta (made from maize) oats (oatmeal, oatflakes or oatbran), semolina – including cous-cous (from which it is made), sago and tapioca.

Pasta has become much more popular recently, and there are many types and shapes to choose from. Keep a good selection, and always make sure you have the basic lasagne sheets, tagliatelle or fettucine (noodles) and spaghetti. Try spinach or tomato varieties for a change and sample some of the fresh pastas that you can now buy. Better still, make your own – handrolling pasta, while undoubtedly time-consuming, can be very satisfying, or you can buy a special machine for rolling the dough and cutting certain shapes. You could also buy a wooden "pasta tree" on which to hang the pasta to dry, in which case you might find you get enthusiastic help if you have small children!

Pulses, such as soy beans, navy beans, red kidney and cannellini beans, garbanzo beans, all types of lentils, split peas and butter beans are very important in a vegetarian diet as they are good protein sources, and contain vitamins and minerals. Buy them dried for soaking and cooking yourself, or buy

canned varieties for speed and convenience.

### Spices and herbs

A good selection of spices and herbs is important for adding variety and interest to your cooking – add to your range each time you try a new recipe. There are some good spice mixtures available – try Cajun, Chinese five-spice, Indonesian piri-piri and the different curry blends.

Fresh herbs are always preferable to dried, but it is essential to have dried ones in stock as a useful back-up to use when fresh are unavailable. Keep the basics such as thyme, rosemary, bay leaves and some good Mediterranean mixtures for Italian and French cooking.

### Nuts and seeds

As well as adding protein, vitamins and useful fats to the diet, nuts and seeds add important flavor and texture to vegetarian meals. Make sure that you keep a good supply of almonds, brazils, cashews, chestnuts (in cans), hazelnuts, peanuts, pecans, pistachios, pine nuts and walnuts. Coconut – either creamed or shredded – is useful too.

For your seed collection, have sesame, sunflower, pumpkin and poppy. Pumpkin seeds in particular are an excellent source of zinc.

### Dried fruits

Currants, raisins, golden raisins, dates, apples, apricots, figs, pears, peaches, prunes, papayas, mangoes, figs, bananas and pineapples can all be purchased dried and can be used in lots of different recipes. Though they are a healthier alternative to cookies and candies, dried fruits are still high in calories, being a natural source of sugar.

## Oils and fats

Oils are useful for adding subtle flavorings to foods, so it is a very good idea to have a large selection stored away. Have a light olive oil for cooking and an extra-virgin one for salad dressings. Use sunflower oil as a good general-purpose oil and select one or two speciality oils to add character to different dishes. Sesame oil is wonderful in stir-fries; hazelnut and walnut oils are superb in salad dressings.

Oils and fats add flavor to foods, and contain the important fat-soluble vitamins A, D, E and K. Remember all fats and oils are high in calories. It is worth pointing out that oils are higher in calories than butter or margarine.

## Vinegars

Choose three or four vinegars – red or white wine, cider, light malt, tarragon, sherry or balsamic vinegar, to name just a few – each will add its own character to your recipes.

## Useful extras

Hot chili sauce, soy sauce, tahini (sesame seed paste), yeast extract, sea salt, black and green peppercorns, tomato and garlic pastes, vegetable bouillon cubes, dried yeast, gelatin (gelozone) or agar-agar are all useful store-cupboard additions.

## THE VEGETARIAN FRIDGE AND FREEZER

Thankfully, food manufacturers have wised up to the fact that lots of us love to eat vegetarian food, so it is now possible to choose from a huge range of prepared meals from the chilled or frozen food cabinets. These are excellent standbys for meals in a hurry and they add variety and choice to the diet. Pasta dishes, vegetable bakes and burgers, curries, flans and quiches are just some of the dishes to choose from.

## The secret of success

As with any cooking, the choice of ingredients is of paramount importance. If they are fresh and of high quality, you are well on your way to achieving delicious food. Not only will the flavors be better, but so will the colors, textures and nutritive value. Fresh fruit and vegetables lose their vitamin content very quickly if stored too long, so buy from the freshest possible source, and use soon after buying.

## SALADS

Salads are such a versatile way of eating, and the variety of ingredients is so great, that they can be made to suit any occasion, from the light piquant starter to the more substantial dish served as a main course or the mixture of exotic fruits that makes a delicious dessert.

Salads can be fruity, eggy, cheesy or just fresh green – all are highly nutritious. They are also generally low in calories, if you go easy on the dressing, or use a fat-free dressing. It is easy to make a salad look attractive and appetizing,

mayonnaise too! Cut out all fried foods while dieting, reduce the number of foods that are high in sugar – and try to resist candy and chocolate bars!

**Taking stock**
Besides stocking a selection of ready-made meals, freeze other basics such as frozen pastries (shortcrust, filo or puff pastry); a selection of breads, such as pitta, French bread, rolls or part-baked bread; pre-cooked pasta dishes, pasta sauces, stocks, bread crumbs, home-made soups and sauces, flan cases, pancakes, pizza bases, and so on. All these will be useful when you are short of time.

**SALAD INGREDIENTS**
Make sure you always use the freshest ingredients to ensure a successful salad. Try to ensure that you buy fruit and vegetables at their peak and use them within a few days of buying.

Every salad can be turned into something special with the addition of a few carefully chosen herbs to add flavor and a delicious aroma. For an extra-special salad, add a few edible flowers, which look particularly colorful and attractive, especially when mixed with a variety of salad greens).

## Herbs

The use of herbs in any form of cooking is to be recommended, but in salads the addition of their fresh, aromatic leaves is of special value.

There are so many herbs from which to choose, such a variety of flavors, aromas and colors do not be afraid to experiment. Their flowers can also be used to add color and flavor.

## Flowers

A fascination for flowers as an attractive garnish for salads was nurtured by our ancestors long ago. Apart from the delightful flavor of many, the color contrast they provide is their main asset. Common sense is the best guide to which flowers may be used whole and which should have the petals gently separated from the calyx.

It is, of course, important that the flowers should look fresh and clean, so should they need to be washed, handle with great care and pat dry with paper towels. Store them in a sealed polythene bag in the refrigerator until required.

Borage, primroses, violas, pot marigolds, nasturtiums, violets, rock geraniums and rose petals are all suitable flowers to use, imparting a sweetness and intense color contrast to any green salad. Chive flowers have a good strong flavor and pretty, round, mauve flower heads which

thus encouraging your family to eat fruit and vegetables. It is also often a welcome dish to serve alongside richer offerings.

Supermarkets now stock many unusual ingredients, which can add interest to an ordinary salad. Experiment with new fruits and vegetables, buying them in small quantities to lend unusual flavors to salads made from cheaper ingredients.

The recipes in this book use fresh herbs liberally adding a unique 'zip' to the food. Experiment with them each time you make a salad or a dressing; try marjoram, thyme, chives, basil, mint, fennel and dill as well as the ubiquitous parsley. Basil goes especially well with tomatoes, and fennel or dill are particularly good with cucumber, beet, and salads.

A salad is the ideal emergency meal. It is quick to "rustle up" and there are times when you might discover that you already have a really good combination of ingredients to hand when you need to present a meal-in-a-moment. A splash of culinary inspiration, and you will find you have prepared a fantastic salad that you had no idea was lurking in your kitchen.

## DRESSINGS

All salads depend on being well dressed and so it is necessary to use the best ingredients, and the choice of oil is particularly important.

The principal ingredients in a salad dressing are oil and vinegar with a variety of other flavorings that can be varied to suit the particular ingredients in the salad.

## Salad oils

Oils are produced from various nuts, seeds and beans and each has its own flavor. Unrefined oils have a superior taste and, although more expensive, they are worth using in salad dressings for their superior taste.

Olive oil is the best oil for most salad dressings. Choose the green-tinged, fruity oil labelled 'extra virgin' or 'first pressing' in order to benefit from its distinctive taste and aroma.

Sesame oil has a strong nutty tang and is particularly good with oriental-type salads.

Sunflower and safflower oil are neutral-flavored oils and can be mixed with olive oil or used alone to produce a lighter dressing. Mayonnaise made with a combination of one of these oils and olive oil has a lighter consistency than from the olive oil alone.

Walnut and hazelnut oils have the most wonderful flavor and aroma, and are usually mixed with olive oil in a French dressing. They are well worth their higher price and are especially good with slightly bitter salad plants such as endive, radiccio or spinach.

## Vinegars

Vinegars such as wine, cider, sherry or herb-flavored are essential for a good dressing. Malt vinegar is far too harsh and overpowers the subtle balance of the dressing. Lemon juice may be used and is often preferable if the salad is fruit-based.

Cider vinegar is reputed to contain many healthy properties and valuable nutrients. It has a light, subtle flavor redolent of the fruit it is made from.

Wine vinegar is the one most commonly used for French dressing; either red or white will do.

Sherry vinegar has a rich mellow flavor which blends well with walnut and hazelnut oils, but which is equally good by itself.

Flavored vinegars can be made from cider and wine vinegar. To do this, steep your chosen ingredient in a small bottle of vinegar for anything up to 2 weeks. Particularly good additions are basil, tarragon, garlic, thyme, mint or rosemary. Raspberry wine vinegar can be made by adding about 12 raspberries to a bottle of vinegar.

Balsamic vinegar is dark and mellow with a sweet/sour flavor. It is expensive but you need only a few drops or at most a teaspoonful to give a wonderful taste. It is made in the area around Modena in Italy.

## Mustards

Mustards are made from black, brown or white mustard seeds which are ground, mixed with spices and then, usually, mixed with vinegar.

Meaux mustard is made from mixed mustard seeds and has a grainy texture with a warm, spicy taste.

Dijon mustard, made from husked and ground mustard seeds, is medium-hot and has a sharp flavor. Its versatility in salads and with barbecues makes it an ideal mustard for the vegetarian. It is made in Dijon, France, and only mustard made there can be labelled as such.

German mustard is mild sweet/sour and is best used in Scandinavian and German salads.

## SALAD GREENS

Round or cabbage lettuce is the one most familiar to us all. I try to avoid the hothouse variety as the leaves are limp and floppy.

### Arugula

The young green leaves of this plant have a distinctive warm peppery flavor and are delicious in green salads.

### Chicory

A slightly bitter-tasting but attractive curly-leaved salad plant. There are two varieties; the curly endive (frisée) which has a mop head of light green frilly leaves and the Batavia endive (escarole) which has broader, smoother leaves. Before they mature, both varieties have their leaves tied together to blanch the centers, which produces tender, succulent leaves.

### Chinese leaves

These are a most useful salad ingredient available in the the fall and winter months. Shred them fairly finely and use them as a base, adding bean shoots and leaves such as watercress or dandelion.

### Endive

This is available from fall to spring and, with its slightly bitter flavor, makes an interesting addition to winter salads. Choose firm, tightly packed cones with yellow leaf tips. Avoid any with damaged leaves or leaf tips that are turning green as they will be rather too bitter. Red endive is also available, mostly imported from Holland.

should be separated into florets before sprinkling over the salad.

## SALAD DRESSINGS

Make up a large bottle of your favorite dressing. Here are some recipes for you to try:

### Sesame Dressing

A piquant dressing with a rich creamy texture.

*2 tbsp sesame paste (tahini)*
*2 tbsp cider vinegar*
*2 tbsp medium sherry*
*2 tbsp sesame oil*
*1 tbsp soy sauce*
*1 garlic clove, crushed*

Put the sesame paste (tahini) in a bowl and gradually mix in the vinegar and sherry until smooth. Add the remaining ingredients and mix together thoroughly.

### Tomato Dressing

A completely fat-free dressing, ideal for the calorie and fat-conscious.

*1/2 cup tomato juice*
*1 garlic clove, crushed*
*2 tbsp lemon juice*
*1 tbsp soy sauce*
*1 tsp clear honey*
*2 tbsp chopped chives*
*salt and pepper*

Put all the ingredients into a screw-top jar and shake vigorously.

233

## Apple & Cider Vinegar Dressing

*2 tbsp sunflower oil*
*2 tbsp concentrated apple juice*
*2 tbsp cider vinegar*
*1 tbsp Meaux mustard*
*1 garlic clove, crushed*
*salt and pepper*

Put all the ingredients together in a screw-top jar and shake vigorously.

## Green Herb Dressing

A pale green dressing with a fresh flavor, ideal with cauliflower or broccoli.

*¹/₄ cup fresh parsley*
*¹/₄ cup mint*
*¹/₄ cup chives*
*1 garlic clove, crushed*
*²/₃ cup natural yogurt*
*salt and pepper*

Remove the stalks from the parsley and mint and put the leaves in a blender or food processor with the garlic and yogurt. Add seasoning to taste. Blend until smooth, then store in refrigerator until needed.

## Iceberg lettuce

This has pale green, densely packed leaves. It may appear expensive, but is in fact extremely good value when compared with other lettuces by weight. It has a fresh, crisp texture and keeps well in the refrigerator.

## Lamb's lettuce (corn salad)

This is so called because its dark green leaves resemble a lamb's tongue. It is also known as corn salad and the French call it *mâche*. It is well worth looking out for when it is in season both for its flavor and its appearance.

## Oak leaf (Feuille de chêne)

This red-tinged, delicately flavored lettuce is good when mixed with other leaves, both for the contrast in flavor and the contrast in color.

## Purslane

This has fleshy stalks and rosettes of succulent green leaves which have a sharp, clean flavor.

## Radiccio

This is a variety of endive originating in Italy. It looks rather like a small, tightly packed red lettuce. It is quite expensive but comparatively few leaves are needed, as it has a bitter flavor. The leaves are a deep purple with a white contrasting rib and add character to any green salad.

## Romaine lettuce

This is a superb crisp variety used especially in Caesar salad. It has long, narrow, bright green leaves.

## Watercress

This has a fresh peppery taste that recommends it to many salads. It is available throughout the year, though it is less good when flowering, or early in the season when the leaves are small.

## Preparation of salad greens

Whichever salad greens you choose, they should be firm and crisp with no sign of browning or wilting. Their preparation for the salad should be undertaken with care because salad greens bruise easily.

To prepare, pull off and discard all damaged outer leaves and wash the remaining leaves in cold salted water to remove any insects, then dry them thoroughly. This can be done either by patting the leaves dry with paper towels, spinning them in a salad spinner, or by placing them in a clean dish cloth, gathering up the loose ends and swinging the dish cloth around vigorously.

Dressing the salad too early will cause the salad greens to wilt.

## NUTS

In addition to color and flavor, salads need texture, which can be achieved by combining crunchy ingredients with softer fruits and vegetables, and using pasta, potatoes and lentils to contrast with such traditional salad ingredients as bell peppers, celery, apples and so on. Nuts are particularly useful for adding texture to a salad, contributing a pleasant crunchiness as well as flavor.

Many nuts taste even better if they are browned before use. These include almonds, hazelnuts, pine nuts and peanuts. To brown nuts, put them on a cookie sheet and place in a hot oven for 5–10 minutes until golden brown. Pine nuts may also be browned by placing in a dry heavy-based skillet and shaking over a high heat until golden brown.

## VEGETARIAN FOOD FOR BARBECUES

These are a welcome alternative to all those summertime meat-eaters' feasts, despite the very idea of vegetarian barbecues seeming odd to many people, who think only of cooking vegetable kebabs or stuffed jacket potatoes. Yet there are so many tasty and nutritious vegetarian recipes that can be cooked over hot coals – after all, barbecuing is just an alternative method of cooking by direct heat. Like broiling and roasting, barbecuing cooks food quickly, so it can be applied successfully to all sorts of vegetarian dishes.

The barbecue recipes in this book have all been devised with speed, convenience and appetizing food in mind, so that cooking is less of a chore, and more like fun!

## PLANNING YOUR BARBECUE

Whenever food is being barbecued, there always seems to be a long wait, so have a few dips and nibbles for your hungry guests. These can all be made in advance and kept chilled until needed. Raw vegetable crudités can be chopped and prepared beforehand, too.

Barbecues always take longer to get going than you expect, so allow plenty of time. Don't be tempted to start cooking too soon, or the coals will not be ready. The flames should have died down and the coals reduced to a steady glow before you begin.

Don't attempt to cook for a large party on a small barbecue, as it could take hours to feed everyone! In this situation, it is better to cook most of the food in the kitchen, and either provide only a few barbecued items, or use the barbecue to finish part-cooked foods. Vegetarian sausages and burgers are ideal, as they cook quickly and can be barbecued in large quantities even on a small barbecue.

### Planning ahead

Many foods for barbecuing will benefit from being marinated, especially dishes using tofu or mycoprotein, which absorb the flavor of the marinade. You can buy tofu in four varieties – smoked, firm, soft or silken; use smoked or firm for kebabs, soft for adding to burgers and silken for adding to sauces and dips.

Have your kebabs ready-threaded for quick cooking; if possible, choose flat metal skewers so that the food does not slide as the kebabs are turned. Alternatively, use bamboo sticks – but remember to soak these in water beforehand so that they do not burn over the hot coals and ruin the food.

Make sweet and savory sauces in advance if you can – the Barbecue Sauce, the Butterscotch Sauce for the Banana & Marshmallow Melts and the Hot Chocolate Dip for the Toasted Tropical Fruit Kebabs can all be prepared ahead to be brought out at the last moment.

### TIPS FOR BARBECUING FOOD

First and foremost, treat food for barbecuing with care – it should be kept chilled in the refrigerator or in a cool box, complete with ice packs, until ready to cook.

Light the barbecue in plenty of time, remembering that you will need about 45 minutes for charcoal to heat and about 10–15 minutes for a gas barbecue to become hot enough.

Food cooks best over glowing embers, not smoking fuel, so avoid putting the food over the hot coals until the smoking has subsided.

Oil the barbecue rack lightly before adding the food, to help to prevent it from sticking, and oil the skewers, tongs and barbecue fork for the same reason.

Control the heat by adjusting the distance of the food from the coals, or by altering the controls on a gas barbecue. Ideally, food should not be cooked too quickly, or else it will blacken and char on the outside before the middle is cooked – it needs time for the distinctive barbecued taste to be imparted.

### VEGETABLES

For kebabs, choose a mixture of vegetables that will all cook at the same rate, and cut the chunks into roughly the same size. Choose from eggplants, tomatoes, sliced corn-on-the-cob or baby corn, mushrooms and zucchini. New potatoes, onions, carrots, parsnips and Jerusalem artichokes can also be barbecued, but will need pre-cooking first.

If you are going to serve jacket potatoes, cook them first too – either conventionally or in a microwave oven. Wrap in foil and keep warm to one side of the barbecue, ready for filling with one of the delicious ideas suggested on page 172. Alternatively, you can finish cooking potatoes directly on the grid over the coals, barbecuing them until the skins are crisp and brown.

Vegetables can be cooked in foil packages as well as on kebab skewers. Slice them roughly, sprinkle with olive oil, herbs and seasonings and wrap tightly. Cook until tender.

## HERBS
Have some fresh herbs to hand for throwing on to the coals. They smell wonderful as they burn, and will add extra flavor to your food. Woody herbs burn slowly, so they are good choices.

## STIR-FRY SAUCES

### Soy sauce
This is widely used in all Eastern cookery and is made from fermented yellow soy beans mixed with wheat, salt, yeast and sugar. It comes in both light and dark varieties.  the light ones tend

## SAFETY TIPS
Choose a safe place for setting up your barbecue on a level surface, away from trees, bushes, fences and sheds. Position the barbecue well away from children's play areas and in a place where your guests won't hamper your activities.

Take great care when lighting a barbecue. Buy one of the special gels or liquids for lighting your barbecue, rather than using dangerous alternatives like petrol or methylated spirits.

Keep children well away from the barbecue.

Have a bucket of sand ready to throw over the barbecue in case there are any mishaps and the food and/or grill catch fire.

## WOK COOKERY
Wok cookery is an excellent means of cooking for vegetarians as it is a quick and easy way of serving up a delicious dish of crisp, tasty vegetables and lightly browned, spicy nuts.

The wok is an ancient Chinese invention, the name coming from the Cantonese, meaning a cooking vessel. The exact date of its appearance is unknown, but it has been used in the East for many centuries.

The clever design of a wok makes it easy to use with versatility; as well as stir-frying, it is also excellent for steaming, braising and deep-frying. Its unique shape means that it heats first from the base and then up the sides, enabling the food to be tossed over a high heat so that it cooks quickly and evenly. It is therefore essential to heat the wok sufficiently before adding the food.

## PREPARING FOOD FOR THE WOK
Everything should be prepared before you actually start to cook or the first ingredients will be overcooked before the others are ready to add.

Always read the whole recipe before you start, and make sure everything is prepared and all ingredients are to hand.

Although Oriental cooks tend to use a variety of cleavers for chopping, a good sharp kitchen knife and chopping board will do just as well. All ingredients should be cut into uniform sizes and shapes with as many cut surfaces exposed as possible, hence the practice of cutting on the slant or diagonal, or into julienne strips or matchsticks.

## COOKING TECHNIQUES
There are four main cooking techniques for the wok.

### Stir-frying
This is the most popular method of cooking in a wok. Once the food has been prepared and you are ready to begin, add the oil to the wok and heat it, swirling it round until it is really hot. If it is sufficiently hot the ingredients added should sizzle and begin to cook.

Most recipes begin by cooking the onions, garlic and ginger, because they flavor the oil. The heat may need to be lowered a little at first but must be increased again as the other ingredients are added. Gas probably gives the best results because of the speed of controlling the heat, and the fact that the curved base of the wok fits so well into the hob. Electricity and solid fuel hobs are more efficient if a flat-based wok is used.

Always add the ingredients in the order they are listed in the recipe. While the food is cooking, keep stirring. When you add a sauce or liquid at the end of a recipe, first push the cooked food to the side of the wok so the sauce heats as quickly as possible, then toss the food back into the sauce over a high heat so that it boils rapidly and thickens the sauce. Once the food is cooked, serve it as soon as possible.

## Deep-frying

A wok is usually used for frying crumbed morsels of food or food encased in pastry. The best oil to use is groundnut, which has a high smoke point and mild flavor, so it will neither burn nor impart taste to the food.

If you have a round-based wok, use a metal wok stand to keep it stable during cooking. It is not necessary to preheat the wok. Simply add the oil (about $2^1/_2$ cups should be sufficient) and heat until the required temperature is reached; use a thermometer or test until a cube of bread takes 30 seconds to brown.

The cooking time is determined by the size of the ingredients to be cooked, and it is essential that the oil is hot enough to seal the batter or pastry as quickly as possible without the food absorbing any more oil than necessary. When golden brown, remove with a slotted spoon and drain on paper towels. Serve at once to retain the food's crispness.

## Steaming

To steam food you need a large wok and a bamboo steamer with a lid. The wok needs a little water in the bottom but it must not reach the base of the bamboo steamer when it is in position: stand the steamer on a trivet. Put the food on a plate that will just fit into the steamer and place it carefully in one of the layers. Add seasoning, herbs and flavorings, then put on the lid and steam until tender. Make sure the wok does not boil dry by adding extra water when necessary. The steamer has several layers, which can be stacked on top of each other. This means more than one type of food can be cooked at the same time.

If you don't have a bamboo steamer, you can still steam food in the wok. Simply put a plate on a metal or wooden trivet in the wok with water to just below the plate and cover with a lid.

## Braising/simmering

The wok can also be used as a saucepan and is excellent for making stir-fry soups, for example. Just stir-fry the ingredients in a little oil, add the liquid seasonings and simmer either uncovered or with a lid. With this type of soup the vegetables should still have a good 'bite' to them, so the cooking time is a lot less than with traditional soups.

Pan-frying and braising are speeded up using a wok because of the improved heat distribution. Simply fry the ingredients quickly, then add the stock or sauce, cover and simmer gently until tender. Sometimes it is better not to cover the wok so that the cooking liquid is reduced, intensifying the flavors even more. Whichever method is used, stir occasionally to prevent any possibility of sticking.

to be rather salty; the darker soy sauce tends to be sweeter and is more often used in dips and sauces.

### Teriyaki sauce

This gives an authentic Japanese flavoring to stir-fries. Thick and dark brown, it contains soy sauce, vinegar, sesame oil and spices as main ingredients.

### Bean sauces

Black bean and yellow bean sauces add an instant authentic Chinese flavor to stir-fries. Black bean sauce is the stronger; the yellow bean variety is milder and is excellent with vegetables.

### CHILIES

These come both fresh and dried and in colors from green through yellow, orange and red to brown. The "hotness" varies so use with caution, but as a guide the smaller they are the hotter they will be. The seeds are hottest and usually discarded. When cutting chilies with bare hands do not touch your eyes; the juices will cause severe irritation.

Chili powders should also be used sparingly. Check whether the powder is pure chili or a chili seasoning or blend, which should be milder. Chili sauces are also used widely in Oriental cookery, but again they vary in strength from hot to exceedingly hot, as well as in sweetness.

# INDEX

## A

Almond liqueur cream, nectarines in, 74
almonds: almond & sesame nut roast, 122
 buttered nut & lentil dip, 158
 Mexican bread pudding, 73
angel-hair pasta: leek & sun-dried tomato timbales, 106
apples: apple & cider vinegar dressing, 233
 blackberry, apple & fresh fig compote with honey & yoghurt, 224
 Waldorf slaw, 33
arugula, 233
aviyal, 45
avocados: avocado cream terrine, 108
 fiery salsa with tortilla chips, 86
 guacamole, 24
 pink grapefruit, avocado & Dolcelatte salad, 152

## B

Banana & marshmallow melts with butterscotch sauce, 214
barbecue sauce, tasty, 164
barbecues, 234–5
basil: lemon & oregano marinade, 166
 Provençal tomato & basil salad, 37
 warm pasta with basil vinaigrette, 46
bean sauces, 236
beans, 227, 228
 barbecued bean pot, 194
 bean soup, 14
 deep south spiced rice & beans, 210
 mint & cannellini bean dip, 93
 three-bean salad, 149
bell peppers : with rosemary baste, 128
 Mediterranean stuffed bell peppers, 180
 nachos, 21
blackberry, apple & fresh fig compote with honey & yoghurt, 224
boiling vegetables, 226
braising, 237
bread, 228
 butter-crust tartlets with Feta cheese, 110
 caraway seed croûtons, 102
 Mexican bread pudding, 73
broccoli: tagliatelle tricolore with broccoli & blue cheese sauce, 114
burgers: nutburgers with cheese, 50
burritos, 62
butter-crust tartlets with Feta cheese, 110

buttered nut & lentil dip, 158
butterscotch sauce, banana and marshmallow melts with, 214

## C

Cabbage: Waldorf slaw, 33
Caesar salad, 38
cake, giggle, 221
cannellini beans: mint & cannellini bean dip, 93
caramel: cinnamon baked custard, 70
caraway seed croûtons, 102
carbohydrates, 226
carrots: carrot & cashew nut coleslaw, 205
 zucchini, carrot & Feta cheese patties, 132
cashew nut sauce, toasted tofu & vegetable mini-kebabs with, 94
cauliflower: cauliflower roulade, 64
 Mexican salad, 34
celery: Waldorf slaw, 33
char-grilled vegetables with sidekick dressing, 200
cheese: baked eggplant, basil & Mozzarella rolls, 88
 blue cheese, celery & chive filling, 172
 butter-crust tartlets with Feta cheese, 110
 cauliflower roulade, 64
 cheese, garlic & herb pâté, 105
 cheeseburgers in buns with barbecue sauce, 177
 creamy baked fennel, 130
 grape leaf parcels with soft cheese & almonds, 190
 goat's cheese with walnuts in warm oil & vinegar dressing, 202
 grilled Cypriot cheese with tomato & red onion salad, 196
 herb, toasted nut & paprika cheese nibbles, 96
 melting cheese & onion french sticks, 174
 Mexican bread pudding, 73
 Mozzarella with barbecued radiccio, 186
 mushroom & pine nut tarts, 116
 nachos, 21
 nutburgers with cheese, 50
 pear & Roquefort salad, 58
 pink grapefruit, avocado & Dolcelatte salad, 152
 quesadillas, 66
 Ricotta & spinach packages, 118
 spinach & Mascarpone soup, 102

tagliatelle tricolore with broccoli & blue cheese sauce, 114
 zucchini, carrot & Feta cheese patties, 132
chervil dressing, 23
chestnuts: Indonesian chestnut & vegetable stir-fry with peanut sauce, 124
chilies, 210, 237
 fiery salsa with tortilla chips, 86
Chinese leaves, 232
 spicy stuffed Chinese leaves, 136
chocolate: chocolate sauce, 76
 toasted tropical fruit kebabs with chocolate dip, 218
cilantro, 90
cinnamon: cinnamon baked custard, 70
 vanilla & cinnamon ice cream, 76
citrus & fresh herb marinades, 166
coconut: aviyal, 45
coleslaw, carrot & cashew nut, 205
corn: Mexican sweetcorn relish, 172
 maque choux, 60
 corn salad (lamb's lettuce), 233
 corn tortillas, 18
cous-cous: Moroccan orange & cous-cous salad, 150
croûtons, caraway seed, 102
crudités, heavenly garlic dip with, 163
cucumber: tzatziki with pitta bread & black olive dip, 160
curries: naan bread with curried vegetable kebabs, 178
 Indian curry feast, 121
 light curry dressing, 208
custard, cinnamon baked, 70

## D

Deep-frying, 237
deep south spiced rice & beans, 210
desserts, 69, 80, 213–24
dips: black olive, 160
 buttered nut & lentil, 158
 fiery salsa with tortilla chips, 86
 guacamole, 24
 heavenly garlic, 163
 hot & sweet dipping sauce, 90
 mint & cannellini bean, 93
dressings, 23, 231
 apple & cider vinegar, 233
 basil vinaigrette, 46
 chervil, 23
 garlic & parsley, 168
 green herb, 233
 light curry, 208

lime & honey, 23
 palm heart & papaya vinaigrette, 23
 parsley, scallion & soured cream, 208
 raspberry & hazelnut vinaigrette, 168
 sesame, 232
 sidekick, 200
 tomato, 232
 warm vinaigrette, 208
 wholegrain mustard & cider vinegar, 168
dried fruit, 228, 229

## E

Eggplants: baked eggplant, basil & Mozzarella rolls, 88
 stuffed eggplant rolls, 26
eggs: burritos, 62
endive, 232

## F

Fats, 226, 228, 229
fennel, creamy baked, 130
feuille de chêne (oak leaf), 234
figs: nectarines in almond liqueur cream, 74
filo pastry, 116
flours, 228
flowers, 230–1
French sticks, melted cheese & onion, 174
frozen foods, 229
fruit: green fruit salad with mint & lemon salad, 222
 summer fruit salad, 78
 toasted tropical fruit kebabs with hot chocolate dip, 218
 see also individual types of fruit

## G

Garbanzo bean sauce, Turkish vegetable kebabs with, 193
garden salad, 41
garlic: garlic & parsley dressing, 168
 heavenly garlic dip, 163
garnish, lime, 237
giggle cake, 221
goat's cheese with walnuts in warm oil & vinegar dressing, 202
grains, 228
grape, melon & mango salad with ginger & honey dressing, 146
grape leaf parcels with soft cheese & almonds, 190
grapefruit, avocado & Dolcelatte salad, 152
Greek salad, 182

green fruit salad with mint & lemon syrup, 222
green beans: three-bean salad, 149
guacamole, 24

## H

Heavenly garlic dip, 163
herbs, 228, 230
  barbecues, 235
  cheese, garlic & herb pâté, 105
  green herb dressing, 233
  herb, toasted nut & paprika cheese nibbles, 96
honey: palm heart & papaya vinaigrette, 23
honeydew & strawberry salad with cool cucumber dressing, 206

## I

Ice cream, vanilla & cinnamon, 76
iceberg lettuce, 234
Indian curry feast, 121
Indonesian chestnut & vegetable stir-fry, 124
ingredients, 227–34

## K

Kebabs, 234
  banana & marshmallow melts with butterscotch sauce, 214
  naan bread with curried vegetable kebabs, 178
  smoked tofu & mushroom brochettes, 188
  toasted tofu & vegetable mini-kebabs, 94
  toasted tropical fruit kebabs with hot chocolate dip, 218
  Turkish vegetable kebabs with spicy garbazo bean sauce, 193

## L

Lamb's lettuce (corn salad), 234
leek & sun-dried tomato timbales, 106
lentils: buttered nut & lentil dip, 158
lettuce, 58, 232–3
  Caesar salad, 38
lime: lime & honey dressing, 23
  lime garnish, 237

## M

Maize meal: corn tortillas, 18
mango, melon & grape salad with ginger & honey dressing, 146
maque choux, 60
marinade, citrus & fresh herb, 166

marshmallows: banana & marshmallow melts with butterscotch sauce, 214
Mediterranean stuffed bell peppers, 180
melon: honeydew & strawberry salad, 206
melon, mango & grape salad with ginger & honey dressing, 146
Mexican bread pudding, 73
Mexican rice, 49
Mexican salad, 34
Mexican sweetcorn relish, 172
minerals, 227
mint & cannellini bean dip, 93
Moroccan orange & cous-cous salad, 150
Mozzarella with barbecued radiccio, 186
mushrooms: almond & sesame nut roast, 122
  mushroom & pine nut tarts, 116
  mushrooms in spicy tomato sauce, 172
  smoked tofu & mushroom brochettes, 188
  spicy stuffed Chinese leaves, 136
mustards, 232
  wholegrain mustard & cider vinegar dressing, 168

## N

Naan bread with curried vegetable kebabs, 178
nachos, 21
nectarines in almond liqueur cream, 74
nutrition, 226–7
nuts, 228–9, 233–4
  herb, toasted nut & paprika cheese nibbles, 96
  nutburgers with cheese, 50

## O

Oils, 228, 229, 231
olive oil, 228, 231
olives: black olive dip, 160
oranges: Moroccan orange & cous-cous salad, 150
  orange, chive & marjoram marinade, 166

## P

Palm heart & papaya vinaigrette, 23
papaya: palm heart & paw-paw vinaigrette, 23
parsley, scallion & soured cream dressing, 208

pasta, 228
  red onion, cherry tomato & pasta salad, 144
  warm pasta with basil vinaigrette, 46
pâté: cheese, garlic & herb, 105
patties: zucchini, carrot & Feta cheese, 132
pear & Roquefort salad, 58
pine nuts: buttered nut & lentil dip, 158
  pine nut & mushroom tarts, 116
pineapple: char-cooked pineapple with ginger & brown sugar butter, 216
  giggle cake, 221
pinto beans: bean soup, 14
pitta breads: pitta breads with Greek salad & hot rosemary dressing, 182
  tzatziki with pitta bread & black olive dip, 160
  vegetable medley, 57
potatoes: filled potatoes, 172
  garden salad, 41
  Mexican salad, 34
  three-way potato salad, 208
  Provençal tomato & basil salad, 37
protein, 226
Provençal tomato & basil salad, 37
pulses, 227
pumpkin seeds: burritos, 62
purslane, 233

## Q

Quesadillas, 66

## R

Radiccio, 233
  Mozzarella with barbecued radiccio, 186
raisins: Mexican bread pudding, 73
raspberry & hazelnut vinaigrette, 168
red kidney beans, 227
  deep south spiced rice & beans, 210
  three-bean salad, 149
refried beans: nachos, 21
relish, Mexican sweetcorn, 172
rice, 227, 228
  deep south spiced rice & beans, 210
  Mexican rice, 49
  spicy stuffed Chinese leaves, 136
  stuffed eggplant rolls, 26
Ricotta & spinach parcels, 118
romaine lettuce, 232
Roquefort & pear salad, 58
roulade, cauliflower, 64

## S

Safety, barbecues, 236

salad greens, 232
salads, 29–41, 140–55, 198–210, 230–1
  Caesar, 38
  carrot & cashew nut coleslaw, 205
  char-grilled vegetables with sidekick dressing, 200
  deep south spiced rice & beans, 210
  garden salad, 41
  goat's cheese with walnuts in warm oil & vinegar dressing, 202
  green fruit, with mint & lemon syrup, 222
  grilled Cypriot cheese with tomato & red onion, 196
  honeydew & strawberry, with cool cucumber dressing, 206
  marinated vegetable, 142
  melon, mango & grape, with ginger & honey dressing 146
  Mexican, 34
  Moroccan orange & cous-cous, 150
  pear & Roquefort, 58
  pink grapefruit, avocado & Dolcelatte, 152
  pitta breads with Greek salad & hot rosemary dressing, 182
  Provençal tomato & basil, 37
  red onion, cherry tomato & pasta, 144
  three-bean, 149
  three-way potato, 208
  tomato salsa, 30
  Waldorf slaw, 33
salsas: fiery salsa with tortilla chips, 86
  tomato salsa, 30
sauces: cashew nut, 94
  chocolate, 76
  hot & sweet dipping, 90
  onion & mushroom, 122
  stir-fry sauces, 236
  tasty barbecue sauce, 164
sauté of summer vegetables, 135
seeds, 228–9
sesame dressing, 232
sesame seeds: almond & sesame nut roast, 122
sidekick dressing, 200
simmering, 237
soups, 13–16
  bean, 14
  plum tomato, 100
  spinach & Mascarpone, 102
  yogurt & spinach soup, 16
soy beans, 227
  three-bean salad, 149
soy mince: cheeseburgers in buns with

barbecue sauce, 175
soy sauce, 236
spices, 227–8
spinach: Ricotta & spinach packages, 118
  spinach & Mascarpone soup, 102
  yogurt & spinach soup, 16
stabilizing yogurt, 16
steaming, 237
  stir-fried winter vegetables, 138
stir-frying, 236–7
strawberries: honeydew & strawberry salad with cool cucumber dressing, 206
  nectarines in almond liqueur cream, 74
summer fruit salad, 78
sun-dried tomatoes, 46
sweet & sour vegetables, 53

## T

Tagliatelle tricolore with broccoli & blue cheese sauce, 114
tarts: butter-crust tartlets with Feta cheese, 110
  mushroom & pine nut tarts, 116
teriyaki sauce, 236
terrine, avocado cream, 108
Thai-spiced lime & cilantro marinade, 166
three-bean salad, 149
tofu: smoked tofu & mushroom brochettes, 188
  toasted tofu & vegetable mini-kebabs, 94
tomatoes: butter-crust tartlets with Feta cheese, 110
  leek & sun-dried tomato timbales, 106
  Mexican rice, 49

mushrooms in spicy tomato sauce, 172
  nachos, 21
  plum tomato soup, 100
  Provençal tomato & basil salad, 37
  red onion, cherry tomato & pasta salad, 144
  sun-dried tomatoes, 46
  tasty barbecue sauce, 164
  tomato dressing, 232
  tomato salsa, 30
tortillas, 18
  burritos, 62
  fiery salsa with tortilla chips, 86
  Mexican bread pudding, 73
  nachos, 21
  quesadillas, 66
Turkish vegetable kebabs, 193
tzatziki with pitta bread & black olive dip, 160

## V

Vanilla & cinnamon ice cream, 76
vegans, 226
vegetables: aviyal, 45
  barbecues, 234–5
  boiling, 226
  char-grilled vegetables with sidekick dressing, 200
  crispy-fried vegetables with hot & sweet dipping sauce, 90
  heavenly garlic dip with crudités, 163
  Indian curry feast, 121
  Indonesian chestnut & vegetable stir-fry, 124
  naan bread with curried vegetable kebabs, 178
  sweet & sour vegetables, 53

toasted tofu & vegetable mini-kebabs, 94
  Turkish vegetable kebabs with spicy garbanzo bean sauce, 193
  vegetable medley, 57
  see also salads & individual types of vegetable
vinaigrette: basil, 46
  palm heart & papaya, 23
  raspberry & hazelnut, 168
  warm vinaigrette dressing, 208
vinegars, 229, 231–2
  apple & cider vinegar dressing, 233
  wholegrain mustard & cider vinegar dressing, 168
vitamins, 236–7

## W

Waldorf slaw, 33
walnuts: goat's cheese with walnuts in warm oil & vinegar dressing, 202
  Waldorf slaw, 33
watercress, 233
  cauliflower roulade, 64
wheat tortillas, 18
wild rice: stuffed eggplant rolls, 26
wok cookery, 235–7

## Y, Z

Yogurt: avocado cream terrine, 108
  melon, mango & grape salad with ginger & honey dressing, 146
  stabilizing, 16
  tzatziki with pitta bread with black olive dip, 160
  Waldorf slaw, 33
  yogurt & spinach soup, 16
Zucchini, carrot & Feta cheese patties, 132